Human Interest Stories
of the
Gettysburg Campaign

Scott L. Mingus, Sr.

Colecraft Industries
Since 1981

Published by Colecraft Industries
970 Mt. Carmel Road
Orrtanna, PA 17353

Copyright © 2006 by Scott L. Mingus, Sr.

The author wishes to thank Chris Hunter and Marcia Wilson for granting permission to paraphrase certain copyrighted materials from their collections. Also, the staff of the U.S. Army Military History Institute provided leads on materials in their library and files, as did the Library of the Gettysburg National Military Park. Most of all, thanks to Debi Mingus for her support and encouragement.

ISBN 0-9777125-24

For more information visit our website: **www.colecraftbooks.com**

Or contact us via e-mail at: **colecraftbooks@aol.com**

First Edition

PRINTED AND BOUND IN THE UNITED STATES OF AMERICA

Cover Design by Philip M. Cole

Illustrations courtesy of Library of Congress

Contents

Introduction

Over a thousand books have been written on the subject of the Battle of Gettysburg, many rehashing the same dreary discussions of battle tactics, generalship, and movements of the troops. I was looking for a fresh angle, and began researching stories of individual soldiers and civilians in conjunction with an upcoming full-length book on John B. Gordon's brigade and its service in the campaign. I found dozens of fascinating anecdotes and stories in scouring regimental histories, letters, diaries, and similar works, many of which have been out of print since the 1880s. I visited historical societies, libraries, museums, and other repositories searching for additional material, and, as word spread of the project, numerous people suggested specific sources that they were aware of.

Gettysburg is often told from the story of the armies and commanders, concentrating on the grim and bloody fighting. However, beneath the swirl of combat and the crashing of the guns, the Battle of Gettysburg was a very individual event for the 150,000 or so troops engaged. Many left behind their written records of events and anecdotes from their service in the Gettysburg Campaign, stories that I found both interesting and, at times, humorous or entertaining. Most have been hidden away for over a century in dusty old books on library shelves, or in microfiche collections of period newspapers and periodicals. The time seemed ripe to introduce the modern reader to these stories of long-ago warriors and the civilians that, for a brief period in the summer of 1863, encountered them.

The tales collected in this book are reworded and interpreted in many cases, but are based upon the original veterans' and townspeople's written recollections. Perhaps some are exaggerated or slightly distorted with the passage of time, but they are generally engrained in true adventures and incidents. All provide some insight into the daily lives of the participants, and mark events they considered to be worth retelling. The reader will find humor, irony, and at times, pathos, scattered among the many stories, but they collectively will tell the story of the Gettysburg Campaign in a way that has not often been delivered.

Additional stories and anecdotes will be presented in future volumes. Sit back and allow your mind to wander back to June 1863, a time and place far away from the 21st Century, yet close enough that we still hear the echoes of Gettysburg.

Chapter 1

The Confederates Invade Pennsylvania

Gen. Robert E. Lee led his vaunted Army of Northern Virginia northward in early June, 1863 to invade Pennsylvania, hoping to relieve Virginia farmers of the constant strain of supporting the two opposing armies. The Keystone State offered a bounty of food, forage, cattle, and supplies to be sent south for the army's future usage. An incursion into Pennsylvania might spread panic throughout the North and accelerate cries for peace. Perhaps the Yankees would strip troops from the Vicksburg Campaign to face this new threat to their second most populous state. The war had dragged on for two years, much longer than the vast majority of people, politicians, and soldiers had originally believed it would. Despite a series of brilliant victories by Lee, the South had continued to lose territory to Northern armies, particularly in the West. Early hopes for diplomatic recognition from Europe had since proved frustrating. The South did not have the manpower, infrastructure, or natural resources to carry on a prolonged conventional war. Hence, it was now time to invade the North in hopes of bringing an end to the bloody conflict. An earlier attempt during the 1862 Maryland Campaign had been thwarted at Antietam, but this time Lee's army was stronger and better equipped.

Elements of this army had broken camp near Fredericksburg on June 3 and slipped towards the broad Shenandoah Valley to the west. From there, they could cross the Potomac River and march through Maryland and the Cumberland Valley into Pennsylvania. A severe cavalry clash at Brandy Station (near Culpeper, Virginia) had resulted in a stalemate, but the Union troopers had failed to intercept or slow down Lee's infantry. Screened from detection from the shadowing Yankee cavalry by J.E.B. Stuart's cavalry, the three corps of the Army of Northern Virginia marched onward. As Confederates poured across the mountains into the Shenandoah Valley, they were frequently met by joyous residents, weary from months of Federal occupation.

On June 11, the 6th North Carolina of Col. Isaac Avery's brigade approached Washington, Virginia. At 2 o'clock in the morning, they passed through the town, where they found "many pretty and kind ladies" who lined the streets passing out water for the thirsty troops and offering them best wishes. After a grueling and dusty hike of some 20 miles, the Tar Heels were grateful when they finally stopped for the night, their morale and excitement high at the prospects of the upcoming summer campaign. Where they were heading, none knew, but the cool water and the pretty girls were an excellent start. For many unsuspecting

Confederates, the long road north would end in a sleepy Pennsylvania farm town known as Gettysburg.

Bartlett Y. Malone, The Diary of Bartlett Yancey Malone (Chapel Hill, NC: The University of North Carolina Press, 1919).

**

Lt. Gen. Richard S. Ewell's Second Corps on June 13 and 14 smashed Federal defenses around Winchester, Virginia, opening the Shenandoah Valley for Confederate movement into Maryland and beyond. The fighting, savage and at close quarters at times, marked Richard Ewell's first success as a corps commander, offering promise for what the future might hold. His inspired soldiers swept away the Yankees, clearing out the last major opposition in the valley. Artilleryman Robert Stiles later noted, "The fire of the Federal guns was very deadly and demoralizing, and the captain [Charles A. Thompson] of the battery next on our right, I think the Louisiana Guard Artillery, came up the hill between his battery and ours to steady his men. He was a fine horseman, finely mounted, and might have well served as a model for an equestrian statue as he rode out between the smoking muzzles, and, rising in his stirrups, cheered on his gunners. At that moment a shell tore away his (left) bridle arm high up near the shoulder. Instantly, he caught the reins with his right hand and swung the horse's head sharply to the left, thus concealing his wounded side from his men, saying as he did so, 'Keep it up boys; I'll be back in a moment!' As he started down the hill I saw him reel in the saddle, and even before he reached the limbers the noble fellow fell from his horse--dead."

Robert Stiles, Four Years Under Marse Robert (New York/Washington: The Neale Publishing Company, 1904).

**

An alarmed President Abraham Lincoln issued a call for 100,000 fresh volunteers to join the army to repel the threatened Confederate invasion. Republican Governor Andrew Curtin of Pennsylvania summoned 50,000 men as his share of the overall total. Few men formally responded, as many were not sure if they were to serve only for the duration of the emergency, or if they had to sign up for Federal service for the duration of the war. However, concerned volunteers flocked to local militia units to protect their immediate communities, homes and families. Arrayed with a motley collection of hunting rifles, antique guns, pistols, farm implements, and clubs, these commands offered no real opposition to the veterans of Lee's army, but they provided a degree of comfort to the citizens as they awaited military intervention.

On June 14, officials of Blair County organized home guards under the command of Col. Jacob Higgins, who had previously served in the 125th Pennsylvania. The ranks included a few men recently discharged from the Army of the Potomac who had served under Higgins during the fighting at Chancellorsville. However, most of the other volunteers were either too young or too old for military service, or had been turned down by the three-year regiments for health reasons. Few other than the handful of veterans had ever been in combat. They fortified several mountain passes in the region while stealing poultry and hams from local farmers. Near McKee Gap, campfires built by hungry recruits triggered a small forest fire, which was soon extinguished. Area residents sarcastically dubbed Higgins' erstwhile soldiers "The Chicken Raiders."

Sylva Epperson, A Brief History of Blair County, Blair County Historical Society

**

An unusual group of volunteers responded in Harrisburg to Governor Curtin's plea. Capt. Charles C. Carson and a company of 17 men, the youngest being 68 years old, came forward and presented themselves for military service. Each senior citizen was a veteran of the War of 1812, and they wanted to again serve their state and country in a time of need. A color bearer proudly carried an historic relic, a highly tattered battle flag that had once been borne at the Battle of Trenton by Pennsylvanians serving under George Washington. The old patriots asked for flintlock muskets, then, using colonial commands and formations, marched to the rifle-pits and took their assigned positions. Their bodies may have been aged, but their spirits were not.

Samuel P. Bates, History of the Pennsylvania Volunteers (Harrisburg: B. Singerly, State Printer, 1869-1871).

**

The Mason-Dixon Line separating Maryland from Pennsylvania also separated slavery from freedom. Along this border, sectional feelings were very bitter and many families were divided, and in several cases family members served in the Union army while relatives were in the Confederate forces. On June 15, Brig. Gen. Albert Jenkins' brigade of Virginia cavalry entered Pennsylvania, creating a mixed reaction among the citizens. Sixteen-year-old Lida Welsh was the daughter of the Chief Burgess of Waynesboro, a small town just north of the border. When the first company of Jenkins' cavalry rode up her street, one of her neighbors, a native of Virginia and pastor of one of the local churches, was sitting on his front porch. The captain of the company dismounted and the minister rushed to meet him. They were brothers and they embraced with tears coursing down each face. Other cavalrymen, friends and college mates, dismounted and also warmly greeted the minister. Concurrently, his wife, an ardent Unionist, had shut herself in an upper room and was crying hysterically because of the desecration of Pennsylvania by Rebel feet. Truly, America had become a "house divided."

The Outlook, June 25, 1925, account of Lida Welsh Bender.

7

**

When Governor Curtin appealed to the citizens of Philadelphia to come to the aid of their state, one well-known group of organized soldiers responded. The First Troop, Philadelphia City Cavalry, had a long and distinguished history. It had been formed by financier Robert Morris during the American Revolution to serve as the personal bodyguard for Gen. George Washington. Comprised of some of the City of Brotherly Love's leading citizens, the First City Troop for subsequent decades was particularly noted for its excellent horsemanship and showmanship during frequent parades and reviews. The troopers had briefly seen service during the First Bull Run campaign and had again volunteered during the Maryland Campaign when Lee had threatened Pennsylvania. Now, during the Emergency of 1863, they again volunteered without pay. Arriving in Gettysburg early on the morning of Sunday, June 21, via train from Harrisburg, the gentry soon impressed the locals with their riding skills and starched white shirts with fancy cuffs and garnishments.

However, one Philadelphian suffered a freakish injury that afternoon as he escorted a few Confederate cavalry prisoners to Gettysburg. Some four miles from town near Wenny's Mill, Pvt. Edward White's horse became unmanageable and ran against a tree, breaking the cavalryman's thighbone. An ambulance was dispatched to carry him back to Gettysburg, where doctors set the shattered limb that evening. An embarrassed White with two comrades took the first train back to Harrisburg and then on to Philadelphia to recuperate.

Gettysburg Compiler, June 29, 1863.
Persifor Fraser, Jr., "Philadelphia City Cavalry," The Journal of the Military Service Institution of the United States, Volume 43, 1908.

**

Soon after, Capt. Samuel J. Randall of the First City Troop assigned the unruly bay that had caused Edward White's broken leg to Pvt. Jones Wister as a replacement for his played-out gray mare. Wister, the 24-year-old superintendent of the Duncannon Rolling Mills in Perry County, had finally tamed the steed and rejoined his comrades. After the patrol halted, Wister volunteered to ride ahead a few hundred yards to feel for the enemy. He soon encountered three prone Confederates, who fired at him. Wister zigzagged his horse to disrupt their aim. "Fortunately for me, they were poor shots. Bullet after bullet whizzed through the branches over my head." As Wister suddenly turned his horse, intending to ride back to report his success in locating the Rebels, his saddle turned under him, pitching him to the ground. A dismayed Wister assumed that either he or his horse had been hit, but, to his relief, he found no wounds. Desperately, he clutched the bridle and dashed for safety, running alongside "Count White." After scampering for a quarter of a mile, Wister considered it safe to halt and restrap his saddle into position. Mounting, he sheepishly returned to his comrades.

Jones Wister, Jones Wister's Reminisces (Philadelphia: J. B. Lippincott Co., 1920).

**

That same Sunday, Brig. Gen. Albert G. Jenkins' Confederate cavalry brigade continued to scout the passes in the South Mountain range, as well as procure supplies and forage from farmers and shopkeepers in the Cumberland Valley. In Chambersburg, a few residents "ran off, but most of the people, knowing there was a military force to fall back upon between Chambersburg and Scotland, shouldered their guns and fell into ranks to give battle. Prominent among these was Rev. Mr. Nicholls, whose people missed a sermon in his determination to pop a few rebels." The eager preacher did not get to fire a shot, as the citizens dispersed before the Confederates arrived in force.

Frank Moore, Anecdotes, Poetry, and Incidents of the War: North and South. 1860-1865. (New York: Publication office, Bible house, J. Porteus, agent, 1867).

**

Tragedy struck one Confederate infantry regiment as it crossed over the Potomac River into Maryland at Shepherdstown, West Virginia. An old wooden ferry boat had been pressed into service to convey Ambrose Wright's Georgia brigade across the swollen river, just below the railroad bridge. Designed for 50 passengers, the boat this night was carrying as many as 150 men. The first passage concluded without incident. However, as Pvt. William Judkins of Company G crossed on the second round trip, he noted that the craft was now badly leaking. On its third crossing, it suddenly sank and thirteen members of the 22nd Georgia drowned. Pvt. William B. Gray, who could not swim, lived by hanging onto a rope. The river was deep at that point, but the boat did not sink over 3 feet. However, several soldiers died in the ensuing panic, with many clinging desperately to those men who could swim, and the combined weight sank them.

A soldier in Company A jumped out of the sinking boat and successfully swam ashore, replete with his knapsack still on his back and his musket strapped around his shoulder. He never even got his head wet. He told his amazed and mourning comrades that he was raised in the Savannah River and knew how to protect himself. Another lucky survivor was Lt. Charles McAfee, whose legs cramped in the water, but companions grabbed him and took him to the riverbank, where after much rubbing and massaging the cramp was worked out. Most of the bodies were recovered and buried, but some were carried downstream by the swift current.

W. B. Judkins account, U.S. Army Military History Institute, Carlisle, PA

**

When Confederate Maj. Gen. Jubal Early's division occupied Waynesboro, Pennsylvania, on June 22, the irascible commander ordered the bars closed and all whiskey supplies destroyed. Several distillers in Washington and Quincy townships attempted to hide barrels of whiskey in out-of-the-way places, and, in some cases, resorted to digging pits to bury their inventory. Confederate officers discovered most of the hidden stash and smashed in the barrelheads. However, a few "Louisiana Tigers" from Brig. Gen. Harry Hays' brigade found some undamaged liquor and soon inebriated Tigers started robbing citizens of clothing, money, watches, and possessions. A particularly favorite sport was to relieve the Pennsylvanians of their high top hats and other headgear. The Tigers paraded through Waynesboro, Greenwood and on into the Gettysburg region on June 26 still wearing their non-military caps.

The Outlook, June 25, 1925, account of Lida Welsh Bender.

**

The Confederate infantry and cavalry patrols struck terror along their route, and wild rumors spread throughout the countryside that the Rebels were actually devils or demons. Pvt. G. W. Nichols of the 61st Georgia reported that, as Gordon's Brigade tramped through one town, a little girl exclaimed, "Why mamma, they haven't got horns! They are just like our people."

G. W. Nichols, A Soldier's Story of His Regiment: 61st Georgia (Kennesaw, GA: Continental Book Company, 1961).

**

A similar story was told by Pvt. John King of the 25th Virginia (J. M. Jones' brigade). "Some of the Northern people had peculiar ideas concerning us; while we were patrolling Chambersburg, we conversed with people at different places. Some would say: 'Why, we didn't think there were so many people in the South.' And only a small part of Lee's army went to Chambersburg. At another house while conversing one of them looked closely at us and said: 'Why, I didn't know the Southern people looked like our people. You fellows look just like us.' Then Bill Lawhorne, a rough fellow and one of our own company said: 'What did you think we looked like? Did you imagine we all had horns and tails like wild beasts?' It seemed strange that anyone could know so little about the South."

John R. King, My Experience in the Confederate Army and in Northern Prisons. (Clarksburg, WV: Stonewall Jackson Chapter, United Daughters of the Confederacy, 1917).

**

Throughout southern Pennsylvania, gossip and stories spread regarding the outlandish behavior of the fabled Louisiana Tigers. As the Richmond Howitzers passed through one town on a bright sunny day, thirsty artilleryman Robert Stiles rode up to the front fence of a prosperous house. He asked an elderly lady sitting on her porch if he could get a drink of water from her well. Quenching his thirst, Stiles sat on the porch and engaged her in friendly and pleasant conversation. Discovering that the Rebel officer had a sister in New Haven, Connecticut, she brought out a table, pen, ink, and paper for him to write a letter to her, and volunteered to mail it. As Stiles finished penning his letter, a young married woman came to the door to tell her mother that her little son was missing. Searching the house, the two women soon emerged onto the front porch, dragging a pale and violently trembling 5 or 6-year old boy. He had been hiding between the mattress and feather bed in an upstairs bedroom, terrified of the blood-curdling stories he had been told of the Rebels' cruelty and ferocity.

Soon, the genial Stiles had made friends with the child, who was sitting on his lap when the frantic mother announced that she had not seen her elder son for some time. Suddenly a "bright boy of ten or eleven summers" burst into the gate, breathless with excitement and wonderment, and gasped out, "Mother, mother! May I go to camp with the rebels? They are the nicest men I ever saw in my life. They are going to camp right out here in the woods, and they are going to have a dance, too!" The much ballyhooed Louisiana Tigers were passing by the women's home at the time, and the mother was taken aback by her son's new companion, "a bowing, smiling, grimacing, shoulder-shrugging Frenchman, who promised, in rather broken English, that he would take the best possible care of him." The mother hesitated, but having trusted Stiles by now, decided to allow her son to accompany the friendly Creole to the dance. He returned home with a much different perspective of the Tigers, who had greatly entertained him with their song and dance.

Robert Stiles, Four Years Under Marse Robert (New York/Washington: The Neale Publishing Company, 1904).

**

To one Georgian in Brig. Gen. Ambrose Wright's brigade, south-central Pennsylvania was only distinguished for its immense fields of waving grain ripened for the harvest and its "nice large cherries, Dutch farmers, and ugly females." He lamented that "handsome females were much more scarce than Copperheads."

Savannah Daily Republican, August 6, 1863.

**

Col. Clement A. Evans, a pre-war lawyer and judge who was accustomed to decorum and manners, observed that Pennsylvanians along the path of his dusty 31st Georgia "do not impress one favorably." They generally lived in "pretty good style", but the majority was uneducated, apparently possessing little knowledge of the outside world. Some of them had never before seen artillery, and they expressed great anxiety to see the big guns. Evans and his men were considerably surprised at the coarse, profane language of the Pennsylvania ladies. To those Rebels who had never heard a rough word escape from the lips of a proper Southern belle, it was "very strange" to hear these rural Northern women repeatedly curse.

Clement Evans diary entry, June 23, 1863.

**

One Alabama bachelor marching along the turnpike from Chambersburg to Gettysburg with Brig. Gen. John Gordon's brigade kept his eyes on the local girls, many of whom he found to be vulgar and not as pretty as the ladies of Savannah. He thought he had made quite an impression on one young lady, who was "exceedingly obliging" in the way of bread, butter, milk, and complimentary remarks. The soldier had no doubt that he could have "made a rebel of her" had he tried. While she was the most attractive girl in the region, he would not consider her good-looking outside of Pennsylvania. However, as with all Yankee girls, she had a degree of sharpness and wit, as well as great confidence that the Union army would soon drive the Rebels out of her state. As the Rebel said goodbye, she naively told him "to be sure and call and see her on my return if I was not in too big a hurry." The infantryman added, "I did not happen to come back by that road or I certainly should have accepted her invitation."

Mobile Advertiser & Register, August 9, 1863.

**

Brig. Gen. John Gordon after the war recalled how some of his soldiers found a "legal" way to get around Robert E. Lee's strict orders to respect private property. Camping in the dark in open pastoral country, the Georgians ascertained that there was no wood nearby for campfires. Several soldiers directly appealed to Gordon for permission to burn a few rails from an old-fashioned fence near the camp. The general agreed, but they could only take the top layer of rails, as the barrier would still be high enough to answer the farmer's purpose. When morning came, the fence had nearly all disappeared, and each man declared that he had taken only the top rail. To Gordon, it was "a case of adherence to the letter and neglect of the spirit; but there was no alternative except good-naturedly to admit that my men had gotten the better of me that time."

John B. Gordon, Reminiscences of the Civil War. (New York: Charles Scribner's Sons; Atlanta: Martin & Hoyt Co., 1904)

**

As Brig. Gen. Joseph Kershaw's South Carolina brigade crossed the Mason-Dixon Line, the front of the column halted in middle of the road, their forward progress blocked by a delegation of "quaint old Quaker settlers" who apparently had little fear of the invading army. They commanded, in the name of God, "So far thou canst go, but no farther." Satisfied that they had delivered God's warning to the Rebels, the faithful, although naïve, Quakers soon returned to their homes. Needless to say, the brigade continued onward, ignoring the laughable command of the pious Pennsylvanians.

D. Augustus Dickert, History of Kershaw's Brigade. (Newberry, SC: Elbert H. Aull Co., 1899).

**

When Junius Daniel's North Carolina brigade entered Greencastle, Pennsylvania, "It seemed that all of the Pennsylvania Dutch for a hundred miles around about had come to look glum at our audacity in venturing so far in their midst." Staff officer Wharton Green accompanied his old friend Col. John T. Mercer into town, where they stopped at a house and demanded a little liquid refreshment. The German owner soon produced a wash pitcher filled with whiskey. Mercer poured a drink and was about to toss it down when Green stopped him. Remarking that he had heard "when in the enemy's country and partaking of his hospitality it is advisable to make your host drink the first toast," he turned and said, "My friend, kindly drink to the health of President Davis, General Lee, and the Confederate cause!"

The Dutchman's countenance fell at once as he replied, "I have not drank the viskey for twenty years or more!" Suspicious that perhaps the alcohol had been poisoned, Colonel Mercer drew his revolver and intoned, "If you have not drank the 'viskey' for one hundred years, you shall drink that toast!" The frightened Pennsylvanian rejoined, "Oh, do not shoot me; I vill drink the toast." Finally satisfied that the elixir was safe to drink, Green and Mercer soon followed suit. As they left, their host gave each Rebel a bottle to take back to their camp.

Wharton J. Green, Recollections and Reflections: An Auto of Half a Century or More (Raleigh, NC: Edwards and Broughton Printing Company, 1906).

**

The Commissary Sergeant for the 5th Alabama Battalion of infantry, William Fulton, rode into Pennsylvania marveling at the similarity of the farms and farmhouses, all made after the same pattern. In many cases, he judged the barns, many of which were topped by a large bell, to be more spacious and better built than the dwellings of the owners. Being from the cotton field region of Alabama, Fulton and his companions found the clover and wheat fields to be very enticing. He noted, "The horses in the clover fields were great big-footed, clumsy, awkward things, so different from our Alabama horses, and though theirs were a great deal heavier and more suited for draught purposes we greatly preferred ours which were more active and could endure more service without jading."

General Lee had issued very stringent orders against straggling and depredating. Rights of private property were to be strictly respected and there was to be no meddling with that which belonged to private citizens, under penalty of severe punishment. Fulton continued, "Soldiers seemed to consider chickens and fruits of all kinds to be exempt from this general order, judging from the way they acted with regard to these. A soldier ran a chicken under a large stack of wheat straw, and going under after it discovered horses and wagons and other things hid away under these straw stacks to protect them from 'The Rebels.' This was reported to the proper authorities and a search instituted which revealed many things of importance to the commissary and quartermaster's stores."

William F. Fulton, Jr., Family Record and War Reminiscences. (Livingston, AL: self-published, 1919).

**

On June 23, the rearguard of Lee's army, a division of Virginians under Maj. Gen. George Pickett, passed through Greencastle, their spirits buoyed by entering Pennsylvania. Marching "victoriously" through the town, Pickett's bands struck up several Southern tunes, including "The Bonnie Blue Flag" and "Maryland, My Maryland." The soldiers kept time as they marched, and many loudly sang and cheered. When the band of the 7th Virginia played "Dixie" as the regiment passed a vine-bowered house, a young girl rushed out on the porch under the purple morning glories and proudly waved a United States flag. Perhaps fearing that it might be seized, she fastened it around her waist as an apron and waved it from side to side in defiance calling out, "Traitors! Traitors! Traitors! Come and take this flag, the man of you who dares!" Pickett feared that his men might retaliate, as many came from a section of Virginia that was long occupied by the Federal army, who had at times spread destruction and dishonor upon the civilians. He quickly doffed his hat, bowed to the girl, and saluted her flag. His men followed suit, lifting their hats and cheering the astonished maiden, who ceased her verbal assault.

Sallie Pickett, The Heart of a Soldier. (New York: Seth Moyle, Inc., 1913).

**

The natives continually amused the Confederate soldiers, many of whom had never before ventured north of the Mason-Dixon Line. According to an article in a newspaper in Franklin County, Pennsylvania (a region with a diverse mixture of people of German, English and Scotch-Irish descent), "Some of the border State, and most of the more southern rebels, have rather peculiar conceptions of the Pennsylvania Dutch. Quite a number were astonished to find our people speaking English, as they supposed that the prevalent language was the German. At first when they attempted derisive remarks, they would imitate the broken English of the Germans; and judging from Ewell's demand for 25 bbls. of sourkraut at a season when it is unknown in any country, even the commanding officers must have considered our people as profoundly Dutch. It would require an intensely Dutch community to supply sourkraut in July."

Franklin Repository, July 15, 1863.

**

Many frightened citizens left the southern tier of Pennsylvania for safer environs. Others hastily hid their valuables, and then led their livestock and horses to the woods or, in many cases, across the Susquehanna River. Acts of kindness were abundant, as well as occasional mischief. Thirteen-year-old Billy Bayly of Gettysburg later recalled how his family drove their horses to Harrisburg and took up temporary quarters with a Dauphin County farmer. The party of six men and two boys repaid the farmer's generosity by helping him harvest his bumper crop of wheat. When word came that no enemy threatened the immediate vicinity of Gettysburg, the Baylys returned home several days later. To their surprise and pleasure, they discovered that their own wheat had been cut and stacked by a similar group of "skedaddlers" from Maryland who had stayed on their farm.

William Hamilton Bayly account, Gettysburg National Military Park

**

Meanwhile, the Army of the Potomac was not idle, but was finally moving to intercept Lee. Rear guard units from the Confederate Army of Northern Virginia at times skirmished with the oncoming Yankees. On June 25, shortly after marching over the Thoroughfare Gap near Haymarket, Virginia, the rear of the 1st Minnesota's column came under fire from a battery of Rebel horse artillery that had entered the gap after the Unionists had passed through. Several men were killed or wounded, and the regiment's colonel, William Colville, had his horse killed from under him. The veteran soldiers, however, were amused by the crowd of noncombatants that often accompanied the fighting men, often staying well to the rear to avoid danger. Not expecting an attack from the same mountain pass they had recently descended, the crowd of sutlers, surgeons, chaplains, and black servants "broke and rushed, in terror and disorder, from the vicinity of the rapidly bursting shells," throwing aside anything that would encumber their escape. The soldiers "shouted with glee" watching the "ludicrous" panic. Then, they resumed their martial duties, forming a strong skirmish line that drove away the Confederate artillery and its escorting cavalry detail. They resumed the march, and several of the noncombatants were no longer to be seen.

Minnesota in the Civil and Indian Wars 1861-1865. Minneapolis: State of Minnesota, 1891.

**

Lt. William Lochren of the 1st Minnesota was greatly amused by the antics of his servant Tobe, a young "contraband" who carried in a large basket, usually on his head, the provisions and mess implements of Colonel Colville, Lochren, and one other officer. Tobe was marching that morning "in unusual pride, in a new pair of coarse cotton pants having up-and-down stripes of bright yellow, blue, and white." He started running with the others at the first shot, but at the scream of every fresh shell would throw himself on the ground, grasping his load and running again after the explosion. A strong skirmish line soon drove off the Rebel artillery and after going on three or four miles, Lochren found Tobe was the only servant who had carried off his load, the rest having been hastily discarded in the panic. But his gaudy pants had given place to ragged blue. Tobe told an inquisitive Lochren that the new pants were "too bright." In his mind, the Rebs saw them and didn't fire at nothing else, but just those pants.

William Lochren, "The First Minnesota at Gettysburg," Glimpses of the Nation's Struggle, Minnesota MOLLUS, Volume 3, January 1890.

**

As the Army of the Potomac headed northward, it was joined by several commands that had recently been engaged in other duties, including two brigades of the Pennsylvania Reserves that left the Washington defenses to rejoin the main army (they had fought with distinction in several previous campaigns). Not everyone was as eager to chase Lee, however. In one case, a portion of a regiment essentially mutinied and refused to serve in the field. The First Regiment Eastern Shore Maryland Volunteers had been recruited in 1861 for three years. They had received assurances from the recruiting officers, under the authority of the Secretary of War, that they were to serve only on the Eastern Shore of the Chesapeake Bay as a home guard. With the public emergency created by the Rebel invasion in June of 1863, Brig. Gen. Henry Lockwood ordered the scattered home guard commands to rendezvous at Point Lookout on the western shore, and from there, to proceed to Baltimore for duty in a newly formed brigade.

Nearly all the men complied, except 61 non-commissioned officers and privates of Company K, who refused to obey the direct order, citing the strict circumstances of their service agreement when they enlisted. The remaining 30 men of that company, under command of their captain, proceeded to Baltimore with the rest of the regiment and subsequently marched to Monocacy, where the erstwhile home guards became attached to the Army of the Potomac's Twelfth Corps. The malcontents were eventually ordered to turn in their arms and accoutrements to the ordnance officer of the Eighth Corps at Baltimore. They all received dishonorable discharges from the service of the United States, but were provided free transportation back to their homes in Somerset County. Undoubtedly some cheated death or injury, but the former soldiers were labeled as cowards for missing Gettysburg.

The War of the Rebellion: A Compilation of the Official Records of the Union and Confederate Armies, 70 volumes in 4 series. Washington, D.C.: United States Government Printing Office, 1880-1901. Volume 39, The Gettysburg Campaign.

**

On June 21, the 149th Pennsylvania of Col. Roy Stone's First Corps brigade was encamped in the Loudoun Valley when a brisk cavalry battle occurred five miles to the west at Aldie, Virginia. The regiment was ordered into battle line, but was not required to repel the Rebels. Returning to their campsite, the soldiers cooked supper and relaxed. A guard was placed on a local farmer's beehive, but when dawn broke, the hive and all the honeybees were mysteriously missing. Another night, a detail "guarded" another farmer's stable, which was filled with fine calves. The guards could not resist the temptation of fresh meat and soon butchered a couple of the calves and divided the booty among their comrades, who ate well that evening. The owner raised a ruckus, and bitterly complained to the commanding officer about this injustice. The quick-thinking corporal of the guard sent a quarter of veal to headquarters. The bribe worked, and the guards were not punished for their transgression of the rule against thievery.

As the regiment marched northward, Capt. James Glenn, the provost marshal, offered his horse to any man who was too exhausted or ill to walk. If the soldier preferred, he could instead load the horse with his knapsack, arms, or other accoutrements to lighten the burden for the day's hike. Soon, Glenn's horse became an unofficial pack animal for the regiment. By evening, the horse would come into camp arrayed with an assortment of backpacks; quarters of beef, hogs, or sheep; as well as all kinds of poultry. The delicacies would be dressed and cooked over the Pennsylvanians' campfires that night, and the routine would be repeated the next day as long as the regiment was in Virginia.

John W. Nesbit, General History of Company D, 149th Pennsylvania Volunteers and Personal Sketches of the Members. (Oakdale, PA: Oakdale Printing and Publishing Co., 1908).

**

By nightfall each day of the grueling march, the soldiers were quite exhausted and normally fell sound asleep quite quickly, ignoring the snoring and the sounds of the nighttime. The assistant adjutant general of the Second Corps, Francis Walker, had laid down one evening with the rest of the rear guard of that corps and was getting a well deserved rest. As he later related, "About midnight the bivouac of the 2nd Division was rudely disturbed by hideous outcries, followed by the noise of men rushing hither and thither among frightened mules and horses. Headquarters turned out in dire alarm, and the soldiers, waked suddenly from the deep slumber that follows a painful march, seized their arms. The coolest believed that a band of guerillas hanging upon the flanks of the column had taken advantage of the

17

darkness to dash among the sleeping troops. At last it turned out that all the fright sprang from a soldier being seized with a nightmare from which he waked screaming."

Francis A. Walker, History of the Second Corps of the Army of the Potomac. (New York: Charles Scribner's Sons, 1886).

**

As usual for the armies of the day, straggling and desertion were persistent problems for both sides during the long march to the North. Charles W. Watson had been a well-known comic singer in the Pittsfield, New Hampshire area before the Civil War. Now 27 years old, he trekked northward with his comrades in the 12th New Hampshire Infantry. Apparently he cared more for dancing and singing than for his military duties, for he fell out of the column en route to Gettysburg. Following the battle, he wandered from hospital to hospital playing his guitar to entertain the medical staffs and patients and did not rejoin his regiment for some time. He was brought before a court-martial to explain why be had fallen out of the ranks during the march to Gettysburg. His quick-witted reply was "to guard the rear of the army from surprise." When challenged as to why he had also skipped the fighting at Chancellorsville, he remarked that he went back "to care for the wounded, surely you would not condemn a man for taking care of wounded men."

Somehow, he only received light punishment, but he was still quite determined to receive a discharge from the army. Stealing a large lot of dried apples and consuming them, he entered a surgeon's tent and anxiously complained that he had the symptoms of dropsy and needed an immediate medical discharge. Failing this ruse, he next complained of rheumatism in his shoulder. His disgusted comrades played a trick on him, handing him a bottle of Spalding's glue and telling him that it was liniment for his ailing shoulder. Watson bathed his arm and shoulder with the liquid, which when dry, cemented his shirt to his skin for several weeks. Watson was forced to join another regiment to serve out his military time before he could return to Pittsfield and resume his career as a singer.

H. L. Robinson, History of Pittsfield, N. H. in the Rebellion (Pittsfield, NH: self published, 1893).

**

The 118th Pennsylvania was known as the "Corn Exchange Regiment," as it had been sponsored by the Philadelphia trading institution. It had received a rude baptism of fire at Shepherdstown during the closing days of the Maryland Campaign, where the regiment had tumbled back across the Potomac River after a charge by A. P. Hill's veterans. Dozens of men had drowned in the scramble and hundreds more were wounded or injured. Now, the regiment was more seasoned and combat experienced. They brought up the rear of their brigade's line of march as they neared Gettysburg, with orders to force any skulkers or deserters back into the ranks, as well as any noncombatants that could carry a weapon. They forced the regimental barber to pick up a musket, as well as some teamsters.

Soon, they encountered an Irishman from a New York regiment who refused to budge. Two soldiers were ordered to level their bayonets at the malcontent and run him through if he did not rejoin the ranks. Judging the man to be a good-natured and friendly fellow, the Pennsylvanians did not want to kill him. The commander of the Fifth Army Corps, Maj. Gen. George Sykes, rode up and watched the episode for some time. Satisfied that the guards had exhausted their verbal entreaties and also not wanting the man shot, Sykes ordered the captain of the guard to leave the man to him, and he would get him moving. Sykes repeatedly lashed the man with his riding whip, inflicting "several smart blows" and ordering him to resume the march northward at the double quick. The Irishman, although headstrong and obstinate, apparently still had a sense of humor about him, even while being publicly whipped by a corps commander. He turned his head to look at Sykes, and with all seriousness inquired, "I say, gineral, 'ave ye any tobacky about ye?" The soldiers roared with laughter, as did Sykes. Still laughing as he rode away, the veteran general remarked, "Captain, let that man go: I'll be responsible for him."

History of the 118th Pennsylvania Volunteers: Corn Exchange Regiment… (Philadelphia: J. L. Smith, 1905).

**

The heat and humidity along the route of march affected soldiers from both armies. While overjoyed at returning to their native state, the 148th Pennsylvania of the First Corps endured a very hard march from Falmouth, Virginia, to Gettysburg. Men dropped from the ranks periodically, suffering from a variety of ailments. William Mackey, a pre-war carpenter, suffered a sun stroke so severe that it left him with nervous prostration and partial paralysis for the rest of his life. He had to abandon his outdoor work as a carpenter, and instead pursue indoor work planing doors in a factory. It also left him vulnerable to temporary sun blindness. While not counted in the lengthy lists of those men maimed for life by shot and shell at Gettysburg, Mackey and hundreds more soldiers suffered permanent health issues resulting from the long marches to and from the battlefield.

Civil War Pension Records, National Archives, Soldier's Certificate 140133.

**

Communications in the Civil War era were mostly by telegraph, written letter, or by personal observation and word of mouth. Likewise, enemy troop movements, morale levels, manpower, armament had to be judged by rather crude standards at times, including the eyewitness testimony of spies and scouts. During the campaigns leading up to Gettysburg, the camps of the 3rd Wisconsin infantry were often visited by a wizened "little man with a sandy face." Purporting to be a peddler of patriotic tunes, the stranger sold copies of lively music that he had written, and taught the words to the soldiers. Soon, his airs were being sung around campfires and on the march. The "singing old rhymester" gained free run of all

19

the camps and was granted permission to come and go as he pleased. Col. Thomas Ruger suspected that the minstrel was taking more than a usual interest in the affairs of the regiment, but could not convince anyone at brigade headquarters that things were amiss. As the regiment marched from Frederick, Maryland, toward Pennsylvania, the men were stunned to see the body of the popular singer dangling from a tree limb in the morning light. He had finally aroused suspicion at the right levels of army command and had apparently been searched, with enough evidence of his spying found to warrant his execution.

Edward E. Bryant, History of the Third Regiment of Wisconsin Veteran Volunteer Infantry 1861-1865. (Madison, Wisconsin, 1894).

**

On June 26, the 114th Pennsylvania ("Collis's Zouaves") reached Point of Rocks, Maryland, during its northward trek in pursuit of Lee's army. The hungry and footsore soldiers discovered that the loyal Maryland women had been busily baking "horrid pies, and cakes that were even worse." However, the boys eagerly snapped them up even at high prices, as they were glad for any kind of change from their routine of munching on hardtack. They also bought plenty of onions, which were also sold on the "gold premium principle."

Two days later, the dusty regiment tramped through Middletown and Frederick, still inexorably heading north to an unknown destiny. All along the route of their march, ladies waved handkerchiefs, and little red, white, and blue emblems were boldly displayed as a greeting of the Union army's coming. These "noble women and lovely girls" brought out cooling spring water in buckets, making the hard march less wearisome. When the band struck up "John Brown's Body," they chimed in and sang the melody with great feeling. At one point, the women threw bouquets of flowers and cheered the soldiers onward. A kindhearted old man brought them a quantity of tobacco. Another, thinking they needed something stiff to keep them in good spirits, brought out a flask of whiskey, remarking, "You boys must want something like this to keep the wind up." The grateful soldiers assured their benefactor that the "potion came at a very opportune time," as they were pretty well played out.

Frank Rauscher, Music on the March, 1862 – '65, with the Army of the Potomac. 114th Regt. P. V., Collis' Zouaves. (Philadelphia: Press of Wm. F. Fell & Co., 1892).

**

Frederick became a quite popular city with the marching Union columns. The town featured a wide selection of bars, taverns and restaurants that served alcohol. Capt. George Thayer of the 2nd Massachusetts later related, "Two features of our march through Frederick come to me with vivid impression - the enthusiasm of the people as we passed through their streets with such cheering and displays of the American flag as our men had not witnessed since the days when they marched from home; and the general drunkenness of the army. I know nothing of the sobriety of the officers; certainly those of my acquaintance had too much anxiety to get their men safely out of the town to stop for any hilarity. But abundant whisky, sold on every hand despite the vigilance of the provost-guard, thrust upon the men by well-meaning citizens, put into the midst of our companions as we marched, and drank before we could break the bottles, which we did most promptly and inexorably, threatened a general demoralization of the rank and file, and did leave hundreds of them within my limited observation reeling in the streets, lying in the ruts in perilous proximity to artillery wheels, or snoring by the roadsides far beyond the town."

George A. Thayer, "Gettysburg, As We Men on the Right Saw It," Sketches of War History, Ohio MOLLUS, Volume 2

**

Acts of kindness towards the oncoming Union forces were frequent in Maryland and southern Pennsylvania. As the regulars of George Sykes' Fifth Army Corps marched from Frederick to Union Mills (not far from the Mason-Dixon Line), one woman stood all day at her kitchen table making "the celebrated Maryland biscuits." As soon as each batch was baked and the pans cool enough to handle, she sent them outside with her children. They stood by the gateway, handing out two or three biscuits to each soldier that wanted some.

William H. Powell, The Fifth Army Corps (Army of the Potomac): A Record of Operations During the Civil War... (New York: G. P. Putnam's sons, 1896).

**

Shortly after navigating the 1,900-foot high Cashtown Gap on June 26, Maj. Gen. Jubal Early split his Confederate division while descending the eastern slope of South Mountain. Scouts had informed him that felled trees partially obstructed the turnpike leading through Cashtown to Gettysburg. The town was rumored to be defended by a Federal force, although Early could get no definite information as to its size. He decided to split his command, sending a portion under John Gordon down the turnpike to Gettysburg while he led the bulk of the division on a dirt road parallel to the north. Heavy overnight rains had since diminished, but the road had become very muddy, drastically slowing his column. Pausing at a nearby tavern, General Early dismounted and went inside. As he conversed with some ladies who were drinking tea, Early noticed a large map of Adams County hanging on a wall. He took his knife, cut the canvas from its frame, and stuck it in his coat pocket. He remarked, "I need this more than you do" as he exited the building with the prize. He calmly mounted his horse and rode off, leaving the astonished ladies speechless.

Emmitsburg (Maryland) Historical Society files

With the threat of the Rebel invasion now turned to reality, Governor Curtin had again called for volunteers. Enough men were raised to form seven regiments of emergency militia. He dispatched one of these, the 26th Pennsylvania Volunteer Militia, to Gettysburg to help protect the nexus of roads that radiated from the borough in every direction like the spokes of a wagon wheel. One company (primarily college students) had been raised in Gettysburg and another in nearby Hanover. A railroad accident in Adams County delayed the regiment's planned arrival on June 25. Shortly after passing through New Oxford, the lead section struck "a poor woman's cow" that had wandered onto the tracks near Swift Run, six miles east of Gettysburg. The locomotive, tender, and several cars suddenly derailed, sending startled soldiers sprawling. The accident tore up several yards of rail and the engine suffered considerable damage. Luckily, only two men suffered minor scratches. The militiamen camped near the wrecked tracks and awaited the arrival of the second section. During the cloudy, cool afternoon, Company A enjoyed pies, bread, and other delicacies brought to them by their fellow Gettysburg citizens.

Gettysburg Compiler, June 29, 1863

**

On June 26, the Pennsylvania militia established a battle line west of Gettysburg near Marsh Creek, but they soon proved to be no match for Jubal Early's combat-tested veterans. Twenty-two-year-old Capt. Frank Myers of the 35th Battalion, Virginia Cavalry, watched as forty mounted cavalrymen of Company E, under Lt. Harrison M. Strickler, a Methodist minister now turned warrior, suddenly charged with "barbarian yells and smoking pistols" in a "desperate dash." Local Adams County volunteer cavalrymen quickly wheeled their horses, without firing a shot, and scattered toward Harrisburg and Gettysburg. As Strickler's veteran cavalrymen advanced a second time, several of the terrified militiamen meekly surrendered. Captain Myers noted that those who could not withdraw "threw down their bright, new muskets, and begged frantically for quarter." None of the Yankees was wounded or hurt, except "one fat militia Captain, who, in his exertion to be the first to surrender, managed to get himself run over by one of Company E's horses, and bruised somewhat."

Frank M. Myers, The Comanches: A History of White's Battalion, Virginia Cavalry (Baltimore: Kelly, Piet & Co., 1871).

**

Confederate cavalry caught up to the remaining militiamen three and a half miles northeast of Gettysburg near the Henry Witmer farm. The emergency troops were so green and raw that most had never fired their weapons before, even in drill. Some were so thoroughly worked up to now actually be facing Lee's vaunted warriors that they placed the powder on top of (instead of under) the Minié ball, thereby rendering their Springfield rifles useless. A few neglected to remove their ramrods and inadvertently sent them sailing at the Rebels. So green was drummer boy Henry Richards that he mistook the noise of the enemy bullets whizzing as sounding similar to a hummingbird. He turned to his older brother Mathias, who being thoroughly exhausted, was prostrated on the ground. Henry asked his brother if he had heard the hummingbird, to which he scornfully replied, "You idiot! You will find out soon enough whether it is a humming bird if it hits you."

Henry M. M. Richards, Pennsylvania Emergency Men at Gettysburg. (Reading PA: Self-published, 1886).

**

Sarcastic Confederate veterans gleefully pursued the fleeing militiamen, who tried several tricks to avoid capture. A quick-thinking young infantryman escaped capture by quickly changing into civilian clothing. Another secreted himself in a meat tub. One hid under a barrel in the storage shed adjacent to the Witmer farmhouse. Those Union soldiers who had been cut off from the main body formed in squads, fighting where they stood, and, in some instances, driving off their assailants and successfully rejoining their companies. However, Rebel cavalrymen soon discovered several poor fellows hiding in the cherry trees and "pricked them with their sabres in that part of the body where a trooper generally half-soled his trousers," ordering them to climb down or be shot. Sue King Black, who lived on nearby Bayly's Hill, noticed students she knew from Gettysburg among the panicked militia, "One of the boys hid under a bed where a Reb found him and asked if his mother knew he was out."

Confederate trooper James Hodam captured six exhausted militiamen who were hiding among the branches of a large apple tree. Nearby, a portly Pennsylvania lieutenant had tried to crawl under a corncrib, but had become stuck. His head and shoulders were under the outbuilding, leaving his lower body exposed. Troopers Charlie Hyson and Morgan Feather struggled to drag the terrified officer out by his feet. To Hodam, "the most fun came when we dragged from a family bake-oven a regimental officer who, in his gold-laced uniform, was covered in soot and ashes. He was a sight to behold." Hodam's comrades in Company F "found a soldier laying on his face as if shot dead. Some thought he was dead sure, but when Charlie Hyson tickled him a little with his saber, he jumped up alright..."

Hodam, returning to his company after escorting a group of frightened captives to the rear, encountered a bareheaded little drummer. The wet, muddy, and exhausted boy was struggling to keep up with yet another line of prisoners. Hodam advised the boy to pitch his drum behind a fence corner, remove his uniform coat, and hide behind some bushes until he could safely return to his mother's home. The lad did as he was told, leaving one less prisoner to be processed by the provost marshal.

Henry M. M. Richards, Pennsylvania Emergency Men at Gettysburg. (Reading PA: Self-published, 1886).
James Hodam (17th Virginia Cavalry) account

As evening approached, Maj. Gen. Jubal Early rode through the Diamond (town square) to the Adams County Courthouse, where guards had formed some of the militia prisoners to hear a speech by the vitriolic warrior. A few townspeople gathered to witness the spectacle. Early surveyed the demoralized captives, a few of which had family in the crowd of onlookers. Crusty "Old Jube" delivered what an eyewitness later described as a hate-filled, stern tongue-lashing. "You boys ought to be home with your mothers and not out in the fields where it is dangerous and you might get hurt." Early in his memoirs would later write, "It was well that the regiment took to its heels so quickly, or some of its members might have been hurt, and all would have been captured. The men and officers taken were paroled the next day and sent about their business, rejoicing at this termination of their campaign."

Jubal Anderson Early, War Memoirs: Autobiographical Sketch and Narrative of the War Between the States. (Philadelphia: J. B. Lippincott Company, 1912).

**

John Gordon's brigade quietly occupied Gettysburg, now abandoned by their militia protectors. The 31st Georgia served as the provost and took turns patrolling the streets while keeping an eye out for stray Yankees, unruly civilians, and any other threats. Guards were posted at the public buildings and stores to prevent looting, and even at a few private houses. All saloons were closed and entry barred by pickets. Some Gettysburg women offered the guards food or water, but they declined, curtly replying, "I must obey orders." As usual, the biggest challenge for the military police came from their fellow soldiers. A few Irish soldiers from Hays' Louisiana Tigers had stacked arms, casually walked into town, and proceeded south along Baltimore Street to the outskirts of town. There, they found some residents also of Gaelic descent who sold them liquor. Soon, a brawl began as drunken Louisianans quarreled with townspeople. The Tigers were busy "beating up the old citizens" when the Georgia provost detail arrived on the scene to put a stop to the brawl.

Isaac G. Bradwell, Confederate Veteran, Volume XXVII (1919).

**

Jubal Early laid a steep bounty on Gettysburg, demanding $6,000 worth of supplies or, in lieu of that, $5,000 in U.S. currency. He ordered John Gordon's brigade to search the town for hidden stashes of food, money, or items of use to the Confederate army. A squad of Georgians approached one home. The corporal in charge informed the lady of the house of their mission, apologizing for the necessity of their visit. She replied that she had few provisions, barely enough to feed her own family for a short time. The corporal mentioned that his instructions were not to take all she had, but to divide the food supply in private houses, leaving something for the family. She escorted him into the kitchen and displayed her meager supply of meat – only about two pounds. The corporal looked at her with some incredulity and remarked that he did not want any of her meat. Likewise the flour, meal, and vegetables were all searched and found to be equally scant, as the quick-thinking woman had previously hidden the bulk of her ample larder. Laughing and joking over her "starving prospects," the Rebels retired without taking a thing.

History of Cumberland and Adams Counties, Pennsylvania (Chicago: Warner, Beers & Co., 1886).

**

Early's men marched eastward on June 27 to York County, where he intended to lay tribute to that prosperous county seat. He sent White's cavalry to Hanover to collect forage, cash, and items of use to the Confederates. Shoes and leather goods were particular targets as Hanover had three tanneries. A party of Southerners approached Joseph C. Holland's shoe store on Baltimore Street. Holland had already sent most of his inventory to safer locations and his store was closed. Waving pistols, some Rebels insisted that Holland unlock the door. "I don't like that, and you are cowards if you continue it," Holland defiantly declared. "If you want to go in my store, I will open it." The angry Rebels promptly ransacked his nearly empty shop, stealing the few remaining pairs of men's shoes.

One thirsty officer entered A. G. Schmidt's drug store, hung his sword belt over a desk post, and demanded a pint of whiskey. Schmidt did not sell liquor, but he took an empty medicine bottle across the street to John Irving's hotel and purchased whiskey for the dumbfounded Rebel. Other cavalrymen came in later to buy soap, brushes, and combs for themselves, and several acquired fine-toothed ladies' combs to send home. The officer, still sitting in a chair savoring his whiskey, told Schmidt that he should only accept greenbacks. Schmidt declared that the soldiers could take whatever they really needed and not worry about payment. He did accept a few Confederate bills, keeping them as souvenirs.

A Rebel handed one merchant a draft on the Confederacy, intending to pay a hefty bill for a stack of merchandise that he had brought to the counter. The skeptical shopkeeper asked if he could really redeem this certificate if he ever visited the South. The cavalryman promptly replied, "It would not be worth a darn." He calmly walked away with the goods, leaving the dismayed storeowner standing with the worthless document still in his hand.

One staff officer wanted his lame horse re-shoed. Locating a blacksmith shop, he asked a group of townsmen standing across the street where the owner was. Blacksmith Peter Frank identified himself and told the Confederate that he wasn't working, it was a holiday. When the Southerner asked why it was a day off, Frank replied, "The Johnnies are in town." He was not open for business with Rebels, but he complied when the officer reached for his pistol holster as a gesture of authority. Entering his shop, Frank fanned the fire with his bellows and went to work. Pulling out a large wad of Federal bills, the Virginian left $2 in greenbacks for Frank's troubles and the new pair of horseshoes. Frank told him that if there were more Rebels with that kind of good money who also needed blacksmith services, the officer should send them his way.

William Anthony, Anthony's History of the Battle of Hanover. (Hanover, PA: Self-published, 1945).

**

The Pennsylvania Dutch farm women had one redeeming value of intense interest to the hungry Rebels – they were good cooks. One grateful Confederate infantryman noted, "Those people make the most delicious bread I ever tasted." The women usually devoted one day each week entirely to baking, making all the bread they expected to need in the ensuing week. The Southerners apparently had reached every farmhouse just after baking day. The astonished soldier sated his appetite on "such oceans of bread I never laid eyes on before. They supplied us with milk, butter, and cheese in the most extravagant abundance."

Mobile Advertiser & Register, August 9, 1863

**

To the north, Richard Ewell's column approached Carlisle on June 27. John Casler of the famed Stonewall Brigade told a messmate, Charlie Cross, that they should find a local farm and secure a home-cooked meal and some fresh cherries, which were in great abundance throughout the region that summer. Hiking about a mile from their camp, they stopped at a large farmhouse that was guarded by a Confederate picket who had been posted to protect the family from thievery or harm. Entering the house, Casler and Cross found that the occupants were an old Dutchman, his wife, and daughter. The Southerners politely asked if they could have some cherries, to which the farmer replied that indeed they could, but they should not take any from the two trees nearest his house, as these were reserved for the family's usage.

To their dismay, Casler and his comrade found that the orchard had been stripped clean by previous parties of soldiers. Ignoring the picket and the wishes of the farmer, the duo climbed up in the trees that were saved for the family's usage. After gorging themselves on the ripe cherries, the Virginians broke off a few heavily laden limbs and walked back to the house, where the family was now seated on the porch. They asked the civilians if they wanted some of the cherries, but they declined. The hungry Rebels inquired if they could get some dinner, but the family refused to feed them, stating that the other soldiers had eaten all the food they had.

While Casler and Cross were sitting on the porch conversing with the old folks, they heard a terrible racket from the back yard. The woman jumped up and ran around the house to investigate the strange sounds. Soon, she returned to the front porch with her hands in the air, her ashen facial expression betraying the fact that something terrible had occurred. She was jabbering away in Pennsylvania Dutch all the time, almost in shock. The farmer and the pair of Rebels raced around the house to see what was causing the din. To their surprise, they found that an old horse had fallen down a cistern, and was doubled up at the bottom.

The old man had taken his best horses to the mountains when he heard the Rebels were approaching. He had not taken this particular mare, as he thought the soldiers would not steal her as she was quite old. He had turned her loose in the back yard so he could keep an eye on her when the enemy arrived, but there had not been a horse in that yard for years. However, it did contain an old dry cistern that was not used anymore, and he had covered it only with some loose planks. They had broken when the mare stepped on them, plunging the horse to the bottom of the 12-foot-deep well. The old folks were beside themselves with concern for their aged horse. The Rebels felt sorry for them, knowing that they would have probably preferred to lose their best horses than this old mare.

Cross once had been a sailor and shinnied down the sides of the well to see what could be done for the stricken horse, who was doubled over in agony in the confined space, but was still very much alive. He asked the farmer if he had any stout rope. He replied that there was a block and tackle out in the barn. The Rebels told him to go fetch it, and also to tell two of the pickets to come to the back yard to help out. The Dutchman went to the barn and soon brought the rope. He also flushed out some other soldiers who were stealing eggs and got them to come along as well. Cross managed to get ropes around the mare, and Casler and the others tied the ends around a sturdy tree. With considerable effort, they managed to raise the horse to safety. They rubbed her legs and worked with her for some time until she was able to stand up and eat some grass, none the worse for her ordeal.

The old folks were rejoicing in the salvation of their horse. As the party of Confederates walked around to the front porch, the farmer quietly took Casler off to the side and said that he and his friend should wait behind when the others left, and he would feed them. As soon as the pickets returned to their post and the egg-stealers had departed, the farmer invited Casler and Cross into his house for dinner. To the Rebels, it was the "best meal we had had in many a day. We parted good friends, leaving the impression that the Rebels were not such a detestable set as he had been led to believe."

John O. Casler, Four Years in the Stonewall Brigade (1906).

**

In the meantime, the Army of the Potomac continued to pursue Lee. The 143rd Pennsylvania of Stone's Brigade crossed the Potomac River on Saturday June 27 and marched the next day to Middletown, Maryland, where they paused and sent out guards. The women and girls of a particular church had to pass through this line of pickets to return home from Sunday School. When one of the guards, Charley Wilson, denied the ladies safe passage, they were very much alarmed and began to cry. The mischievous soldier then told them they could indeed pass, but at the price of a kiss. The ladies obliged and returned home. Later in the day, two other women approached the regiment and informed the soldiers that if any had letters that needed mailed, they would stamp them at their expense and ensure that they were posted. They gathered a large supply of letters (mostly unstamped) and followed through with their offer to mail them.

Simon Hubler manuscript (August 12, 1912), used by written permission of Marcia Wilson. First published in the New York Times, June 29, 1913.

**

Maj. Gen. Winfield S. Hancock, commander of the Union Second Army Corps, had issued strict orders against thievery, with serious penalties for anyone who violated these instructions. One evening in Maryland, he passed through the camp of the Irish Brigade for an inspection tour. Off in the distance, he spotted a stray sheep running at full speed, with a small knot of soldiers in hot pursuit, looking for some fresh mutton for dinner. Hancock spurred his horse towards the culprits. As he neared, he watched the sheep fall into some brush. He cursed, "Blank, blank, you blank blank scoundrels. Did you not hear my orders? Send out the man that killed that sheep! I saw the animal drop! Do not try to evade, or I will have the whole company punished." No one moved forward to admit his guilt in the presumed slaying. Using more vigorous language, Hancock re-emphasized his threat of punitive action. Suddenly, the "dead" sheep jumped out of the brush and raced off. The chagrined general wheeled his horse to return to his headquarters and remarked, "I take it all back. I am glad that you have not transgressed my orders." The sheep, apparently exhausted, had indeed suddenly fallen as if dead from a wound. Recovering, it had taken off to supposed safety. However, Father William Corby of the Irish Brigade later remarked, "To be truly candid, however, I am of the opinion that that sheep did not die a natural death!" Hungry soldiers on the march usually found a way to fill their bellies, major generals not withstanding.

William Corby, Memoirs of Chaplain Life: Three Years with the Irish Brigade in the Army of the Potomac, (Chicago: La Monte, O'Donnell, printers, 1893).

**

On Sunday morning, June 28, Jubal Early with three brigades of his division, about 6000 men, crossed through rural Dover Township toward York. Near the small village of Davidsburg, a number of the locals sat on the wooden fence alongside Canal Road to watch the passage of the lengthy Rebel column. Among the spectators was John B. May, who held a York newspaper in his hand. General Early and his staff were riding near the head of the column. When he saw the paper in the hands of the onlooker, Early asked for it. May complied and handed it to the general. Early immediately began to scan it as he rode along stating, "This is just what I wanted." He expected to find some information of local value in it concerning the whereabouts of Yankee militia.

George R. Prowell, History of York County, Pennsylvania. (Chicago: J. H. Beers and Co., 1907).

Early's men (and later, J.E.B. Stuart's cavalry) were astonished by some of the locals, who would periodically flash mysterious hand gestures at the Rebels. When confronted about the location of their horses, the Pennsylvanians would produce printed tickets purported to have been issued by a secret Confederate sympathizer group, the Knights of the Golden Circle. The unwitting farmers had paid a dollar apiece for these worthless scraps of paper and meaningless hand signals, which allegedly guaranteed that their horses would be spared by the Rebels. Laughingly, the Confederates often knocked the tickets out of the fuming farmers' hands as they led away their animals. An amused Jubal Early would later write, "[T]he purchasers of the mysteries had been badly sold."

Jubal Anderson Early, War Memoirs: Autobiographical Sketch and Narrative of the War Between the States. (Philadelphia: J. B. Lippincott Company, 1912).

**

As the vanguard of Early's division entered York on Sunday morning, resident Cassandra Small spotted "the first ones to appear — an immense number with shovels, spades, pickaxes, hoes and all sorts of tools — carried them like guns. One lady told us she thought that she would see first officers on prancing horses with handsome uniforms, but when she saw these frightful creatures, she raised her hands and exclaimed: 'Oh, my Heavenly Father, protect us; they are coming to dig our graves.' "

Cassandra Small letters, York County Heritage Trust

**

Late in the afternoon of June 28, John Gordon's brigade skirmished with Union militia at Wrightsville, who blocked the Georgians' access to the mile-long wooden covered bridge across the Susquehanna River leading to lush Lancaster County. After a brief firefight, the emergency militia withdrew across the bridge, which was set on fire to prevent Confederate passage. Gordon's brigade could not pursue, as the river level was swollen from recent hard rains. They occupied Wrightsville while awaiting further orders from Jubal Early. Some Georgians had billeted in Samuel Smith's residence. One of his three sons, 19-year-old Silas, had enlisted in the Union infantry to go south to fight the Rebels. The youth had carried a pocket testament that had been given to him as a parting gift. Mortally wounded in a battle in Virginia, he had eventually died in a Confederate field hospital far from Wrightsville.

Now, he slept in an unmarked grave in the enemy's homeland, while Rebels slept in his parents' Pennsylvania home. Samuel and Eliza Smith had fled at the approach of the Confederates, leaving their door unlatched. Returning the day after Gordon's men had departed, Mrs. Smith was stunned to find her dead son's testament lying on her kitchen table.

She trembled as she opened it, finding his name and address inscribed on the flyleaf. A small, but precious part of her beloved Silas had returned home.

George R. Prowell, History of York County, Pennsylvania. (Chicago: J. H. Beers and Co., 1907).

**

On Sunday the 28th, elements of the Union Army of the Potomac arrived in Gettysburg. Col. Russell Alger and the 6th Michigan Cavalry led the way up the Emmitsburg Pike, closely followed by the 5th Michigan Cavalry. The citizens, weary from Jubal Early's previous occupation of the borough, came out in their Sunday attire to greet the blue-clad troopers. Wolverine cavalryman James Kidd recounted the gala scene, "The church bells rang out a joyous peal, and dense masses of beaming faces filled the streets as the narrow column of fours threaded its way through their midst. Lines of men stood on either side with pails of water or apple butter; others held immense platters of bread. Ladies took the slices, covered them with apple butter, and passed a 'sandwich' to each soldier as he passed. At intervals of a few feet the bevies of women and girls handed out bouquets and wreaths of flowers. By the time the center of the town was reached, every man had a bunch of flowers in his hand, or a wreath around his neck. Some even had their horses decorated, and the one who did not get a share was a very modest trooper indeed. The people were overjoyed, and received us with an enthusiasm and hospitality born of full hearts."

These Federal horsemen departed on June 29, heading back into Maryland and again leaving Gettysburg exposed. However, the residents took comfort in knowing that the Army of the Potomac was so near.

Address of General James H. Kidd, At the Dedication of Michigan Monuments Upon the Battle Field of Gettysburg, June 12, 1889 (GNMP).

**

Robert E. Lee, having been informed that the Union army, under newly appointed commander George Meade, was rapidly marching northward to intercept the Confederates, ordered his widely scattered corps to concentrate near Cashtown. Jubal Early remained at York until the early morning of June 30 when he retraced his path back towards Gettysburg. When he arrived at Davidsburg about noon, he stopped at the roadside hotel and tavern of William Julius. Early ordered dinner for himself, his staff and two of his brigadier generals, William "Extra Billy" Smith and Harry Hays, in all, twenty men. At this time, General Early did not know that he might meet an opposing force of Federal troops in the Paradise Valley that afternoon.

While the proprietor's family prepared the food, Early and his brigadiers held a conference in a small room where they spoke in low tones, discussing the military situation.

The staff officers sat in a front room, some of them reading pocket Bibles, for they all knew a desperate battle was soon to take place. These twenty men sat around a long table for half an hour eating their midday meal, which they all seemed to relish. There was very little conversation at the dining table, for a serious air seemed to pervade the entire room all the time they remained. As Early and one of his officers walked out the hotel's front door, they heard the distant booming of cannon toward the southwest. "I suppose a battle has begun," said General Hays to his superior as Early mounted his horse, which was being held by the proprietor. Before leaving the hotel, Early handed William Julius four five-dollar Confederate notes in payment for the twenty dinners that he had ordered.

George R. Prowell, History of York County, Pennsylvania. (Chicago: J. H. Beers and Co., 1907).

**

Meanwhile, the Army of Northern Virginia was widely scattered throughout southern Pennsylvania. In Ewell's Second Army Corps, Early was in York County, Johnson and Rodes were in Cumberland County near Harrisburg. Hill and Longstreet's divisions were between Chambersburg and Gettysburg. The 2nd Georgia of Benning's Brigade was encamped near the base of the South Mountain range. Pvt. William Houghton and two other soldiers received permission to go out foraging for food and supplies. Spotting a distant farm house, they quickened their pace, expecting to "share some frugal Dutchman's ample supply of good things." To their dismay, they noted a half dozen other foragers also descending upon the same house. Assuming that there would be nothing left for them, they looked for an alternative farm. Seeing a clearing on the foothills of the mountain far in the distance, they rapidly made their way across an uncultivated field, but discovered that the farmhouse was abandoned. Noting fresh footprints on a nearby path, they decided to investigate. Soon the path entered a thicket so dense and dark that one of the Georgians proposed that they abandon their futile quest and return to camp, but his comrades overruled him and the trio pressed onward into the gloom.

The Rebel in front suddenly halted and leveled his musket, as did his companions. He had noted a horse fastened by a rope to a sapling about 50 yards ahead. Cautiously approaching the animal, they could find no immediate sign of its owner. Houghton soon discovered the entrance to a nearby cave and called his friends over to examine it. They noted human tracks in the dirt around the opening, which led to an immense ledge of rocks beneath a canopy of fallen trees and logs. Calling for the occupants to come out as they would not be harmed, the Rebels awaited a response, but none came. Finally, against the advice of his companions, Houghton cautiously entered the dim passage. He had proceeded some distance when, around a sharp turn, he was startled to see a pretty girl reclining on a rock, accompanied by a man with a gun in his hand. Luckily, Houghton had not been spotted. He watched carefully for other occupants, but soon figured the pair was alone.

They were quietly conversing as Houghton slipped into a crevice of the rock wall and called out, "Hello there!" The gun-toting man bounded up, striking his head against one of the logs covering the cave. Simultaneously, the girl erupted with "a succession of very healthy and voluminous screams." The man cried out, "Mine Got! We be kilt already, mine Got!" then joined her chorus of screams for several minutes. When the clamor finally abated, a thoroughly amused Houghton finally called out for the man to stuff his hat in his mouth and stop that noise. He would not harm the frightened pair, and if they continued, "they would scare all the wolves and bears off the mountain and run the Rebels back across the Potomac." His joking calmed the occupants, but they trembled perceptively in the shadows. Ordering the man to put aside his weapon, Houghton entered the chamber. He soon discovered that the pair consisted of a fair Dutch girl and her brother, merely an overgrown boy. They had been over the mountain visiting friends when their route was cut off by a Confederate cavalry patrol. Their minds were so filled with terror and fear of the horrible Rebels that they had sought out the cavern, which the boy knew from hunting expeditions.

Houghton, a prewar school teacher, reassured the young people that he and his comrades truly meant no harm. The Confederates led them out of the cave to their horse and then down the mountainside to the place where they had secreted their wagon. Hitching up the horse, the Rebels sent the German Pennsylvanians on their way, "rejoicing and heaping blessing on the heads of the 'repols.' "

W. R. and M. B. Houghton, Two Boys in the Civil War and After. (Montgomery, AL: The Paragon Press, 1912).

**

Many Confederates reported amusing encounters with the local populace, much of which was skeptical regarding the payments that the Rebels often left in exchange for merchandise and food. Near one York County town, the proprietor of a well-stocked country tavern to his dismay watched as ravenous Southerners devoured his entire stock of bacon, beef, and poultry. They forced his wife to use up all of his remaining flour to bake them bread and pies. Soldiers took all of his forage for their horses, and many catnapped on his beds. Perhaps most annoying to the innkeeper, his inventory of 10-12 barrels of liquor had been reduced to a few mere pints remaining as the unwelcome guests finally took their leave, hauling away what alcohol they had not guzzled.

A colonel, perhaps with a tinge of guilt for all the food and drink the men had consumed, loudly stated that it was a pity that no one else had offered to the distraught hotel owner any compensation for his loss. He stepped to the bar and laid down a Confederate 20-dollar bank note, looking around at his comrades as he intoned, "There, my good fellow, take that as my share of our indebtedness." The quizzical proprietor, in a thick German accent, inquired, "Vot kind of monish is dat?" to which the officer calmly replied, "That, Sir, is a greyback; in other words, a note of the Confederate States of America."

"O stranger," retorted the vexed saloonkeeper, "if you hash not got no petter monish dan dat, you'll better keeps it. I don't vont none of it; it is good for nix; no petter dan plank paper!"

"Sir," rejoined the somewhat indignant officer, "I advise you to take it and be glad for the opportunity. You will soon find that it is the best money in the world. Keep it, Sir, keep it, by all means."

"Nein, nein," shot back the persistent innkeeper, "dat monish will never be wort anything here nor anywhere. I would not give von silver thaler for a breadbasket full. I von't be seen mit it in my hand; and if you don't take it along, I rolls it up, holds it at the candle, un lites my pipe mit it." The Rebel quickly snatched up the banknote and returned it to his wallet before leaving.

Richard Miller, The Pictorial Book of Anecdotes and Incidents of the War of the Rebellion, Civil, Military, Naval and Domestic... (Hartford, CT: Hartford Publishing Company, 1867).

**

Many commanders in the Federal army pushed their troops ever northward, hoping to catch up to Lee's Rebels. In some cases, the old adage "haste makes waste" was appropriate. On June 29, the Second Corps made a lengthy march on a very hot and dusty day. At 8:00 in the morning, the 126th New York had forded a small stream just deep enough to cover the men's ankles. An officer had forbidden the men from removing their shoes and stockings, and before the regiment had marched five miles, most of the men had blisters on their feet. By the time the corps halted at 8 p.m. after a twenty-nine mile hike, nearly 80% of the men were widely scattered down the road, many in absolute agony from the painful sores. In Capt. Winfield Scott's company, only 12 men answered the nightly roll call out of 60 who had crossed the stream twelve hours earlier. To Scott's surprise, he had the highest percentage present of any company in the entire regiment. With so many men *hors du combat*, the entire corps halted for a day to recuperate and recover stragglers. In the future, the men were allowed to remove their shoes and socks when there were creeks to ford.

Chaplain Winfield Scott, Pickett's Charge As Seen From the Front Line: A Paper Prepared and Read Before the California Commandery of the Military Order of the Loyal Legion of the United States, February 8, 1888.

**

One Union officer deliberately violated the mandatory order that forced the men to wade through the water. Col. William Colville of the 1st Minnesota allowed his men to cross the same three-foot deep stream on a log, thereby sparing them the agony of marching with wet shoes. His men were exceedingly grateful, but his superiors were not amused. Colville was soon placed under arrest. He would not be reinstated until July 2 when he and his men were needed at Gettysburg. There, he would be wounded in the hip and crippled for life, ironically just before his men charged across a dry creek.

Judge Bert Feeler, Reminiscences of Col. Colville, North Shore Historical Assembly, August 22, 1936 (Files of the Gettysburg Discussion Group).

**

Elements of Stuart's cavalry clashed in the streets of Hanover, Pennsylvania, on June 30 with Judson Kilpatrick's Union cavalry division. Lt. Col. William H. Payne of the 2nd North Carolina Cavalry suffered an ignominious fate, being captured by his own prisoner, Pvt. Abram Folger of Company H, 5th New York Cavalry, in a most unusual way. Folger explained, "While charging at the edge of town and getting separated from our regiment, I was made prisoner by Colonel Payne and was being taken to the rear on the main road. Just outside the town was situated a tannery, the vats of which were not covered and very close to the street. I was walking along beside the colonel's orderly, and as we came near these tannery vats, I saw a carbine lying on the ground. When I came up to it, I quickly took it, and seeing it was loaded I fired and killed Payne's horse, which in its death struggle fell over towards the vats, throwing Payne head first into one of them completely under the tanning liquid. Seeing the colonel was safe enough for the moment, I turned my attention to the orderly, who...was about to jump his horse over the fence to the right and escape that way if he could, but not being able to do so, concluded he had better surrender....I took him in and disarmed him, and made him help to get the colonel out of the tanning liquid. His gray uniform with its velvet facing and white gauntlet gloves, his face and hair had all been completely stained, so that he presented a most laughable sight."

William Anthony, Anthony's History of the Battle of Hanover. (Hanover, PA: Self-published, 1945).

**

As the fighting opened along Hanover's Frederick Street, a portion of the 18th Pennsylvania Cavalry fell back before a sudden mounted charge by the 2nd North Carolina Cavalry. As the Tar Heels surged ahead, they encountered a fleeing wagon, the private ambulance of Dr. Wood, chief surgeon of Kilpatrick's Division. The Rebels began to hack at the canvas cover with their sabers to reveal the contents, piercing the covering with over a dozen gashes. The sole occupant was a hospital attendant named Spaulding, suffering from an illness and very much concerned about the swords hacking away above his head. He crawled up to the front and told the driver, a soldier named Forsythe, to swap places with him. While Spaulding held the reins, Forsythe blazed away with a six-shooter the pair had, holding the Rebels at bay until the ambulance could reach safety.

E. A. Paul, "Operations of Our Cavalry. The Michigan Cavalry Brigade," New York Times, August 6, 1863.

34

**

On June 29, having been informed that the Army of the Potomac was pursuing him more rapidly than he had thought, Robert E. Lee had decided to concentrate his army near Cashtown. Ewell and Early were recalled from Cumberland and York counties and the quest for Harrisburg was abandoned. The following day, the chaplain of Harry Heth's division, J. M. Meredith, and the divisional surgeon, Dr. E. B. Spence, rode from Cashtown into Gettysburg to collect much needed medical supplies. They spotted no troops, friendly or otherwise, on their five-mile journey, but Spence had been assured that a Confederate brigade was indeed in front of them. Tying their horses in front of the first drugstore they encountered, the pair of noncombatants entered and began shopping. Soon, their attention was drawn to a regiment of North Carolinians that they spotted nearby, marching at the quick time. Fearing that the Federals were near, Meredith and Spence joined the column and headed back to Cashtown without completing their purchases.

Richmond Times, April 12, 1896

**

These North Carolinians were from a brigade under Johnston Pettigrew that had marched toward Gettysburg to collect supplies in a train of empty wagons, but hastily withdrew when they spotted oncoming Union cavalry. The horse soldiers were from Brig. Gen. John Buford's division, a veteran outfit with considerable combat success. As the Federals rode into Gettysburg, they were warmly greeted by the citizens. To 14-year-old Tillie Pierce, they offered protection and were her "dearest friends." She and a small crowd of girls were standing on the corner of Washington and High Streets watching the martial parade when her sister began serenading the soldiers with "Our Union Forever." Not all the young ladies knew the words, but all knew the chorus, which they kept repeating until the procession had passed. The soldiers at once began to thank the girls and give them cheers. Battle loomed, but for now, all was merry.

Tillie Pierce account, Gettysburg National Military Park

**

For the citizens of Gettysburg, June 30 would be the final night that the borough would sleep in obscurity. Lydia Catherine Ziegler, the daughter of the steward of the Lutheran Theological Seminary, climbed to the building's cupola and peered into the darkness. Off in the distance on the silhouette of South Mountain she could see hundreds of twinkling campfires, delineating the positions of the Confederates. Below her were the camps of some of Buford's cavalrymen, many of whom were quietly engaged in writing letters to loved ones, some perhaps for the final time. Nearby, a large circle of somber blue-clad troopers were praying, and their words drifted in on the summer breezes, petitioning the

Heavenly Father for protection on the morrow. Still other knots of soldiers were busy singing patriotic songs, including "The Star Spangled Banner." Lydia and her companions descended from the cupola with heavy hearts. War had come to Gettysburg.

Lydia Ziegler account, Gettysburg National Military Park

Chapter 2

The Battle of Gettysburg
Wednesday, July 1, 1863

As elements of Lee's army approached Gettysburg from the South Mountain range, Adams County residents quickly began hiding their valuables. One old man owned a rather modest farmer's inn in town. Having just received a large shipment of choice liquors (whiskey, brandy and gin), Charles Wills feared that his stock would be sacrificed when the Confederates passed by. Not only did he worry about severe economic loss, he had heard the rumors of destruction and wanton behavior allegedly caused by drunken Rebels in other towns. With the Confederates threatening, he did not have time to repack the liquor and ship it to safety in Baltimore. His only real option was to somehow hide it on his premises, or lose it to the enemy soldiers. After anxiously considering several ingenious schemes, he finally decided to go out to his garden as soon as the evening shadows had fallen. There he dug a deep long trench and rolled in the wooden barrels of his precious treasure. He neatly covered the earth over them, very carefully smoothed the soil, and planted the newly tilled ground with cabbage plants. He hoped to give the illusion that his fresh garden was merely in hopes of a profitable crop of cabbage.

When all his wearisome labor was finished, in the morning light he regarded his night's work with smug complacency. He decided to invite one of his unsuspecting neighbors to admire his fine new cabbage patch. The neighbor came, saw, and commended, but had no suspicion that the garden actually hid several casks of alcohol. This was a fortunate omen to the old innkeeper, but Wills still needed a good excuse to explain why he had no liquor on the premises. He had saved out a few gallons of each of the poorer brands. After pouring these cheap whiskies into several empty barrels, he rolled them into an obscure corner of his inner cellar and piled potatoes over them.

Amidst the din and turmoil of the terrible first day of the Battle of Gettysburg, the Union First and Eleventh Army Corps, ploughed by shot and shell, were obliged to yield the ground west and north of town that they had held much of the day. As they rapidly fell back through the town, the victorious Rebels followed close on their heels. The Southerners poured through all the streets, leveled the fences, and entered gardens and enclosed yards. Houses and private apartments were not secure from their intrusion. The inn and the cabbage patch were no exception.

Later, as the victorious Confederates arrived in downtown Gettysburg, one of the first questions when they came upon the innkeeper's premises was "Where is the liquor?"

Looking very serious, the host answered that his stock was entirely exhausted. "That will do for the marines," exclaimed one thirsty Rebel, "but it's too thin for us. We have traveled." Cocking his musket and leveling it at the old man's head, the soldier ordered him to reveal where the liquor was, or he would have no time to say his final prayers. Regarding this as a very careless way to handle firearms, and believing discretion the better part of valor, Wills led the way downstairs to the innermost cellar. There, he took down the elaborately piled up barricades and removed great bars and bolts on the cellar door. He soon commenced leveling the potatoes. The Confederate soldiers, eager for a sip to relieve their parched throats, eagerly lent him a helping hand. Finally the hidden barrels were reached and the liquor brought to light. The foil was complete. No further search was made nor questions asked. The hidden barrels of the choice whiskeys and spirits remained hidden out back in the cabbage patch.

Patiently during those hot July days, while the booming of cannon and the tramp of the armies resounded and shook Gettysburg's dwellings and the volumes of sulphurous smoke obscured the sun in the midday skies, the old man and his son toiled. They cultivated his cabbage plants, hoeing the same ground again and again. The Rebels were constantly passing, their line of battle running just in front of his premises. They were frequently in and out of his house, but they had no suspicion of his secret stash.

The third day was marked by a lengthy cannonade, followed by the terrible din of battle as Pickett and his comrades vainly charged Cemetery Ridge, well south of the inn. The Rebels, who before had been quite boastful and jubilant, suddenly became reticent and their faces lengthened like the shadows. The hot summer night passed and the morning came, the joyous Fourth of July. The enemy soldiers had departed in the night and now Union troops proudly flew the star spangled banner through Gettysburg. Charles Wills no longer had to continue his ruse of cultivating the cabbage. However, heavy rain during the night had soaked through the tilled soil and entered the barrels, ruining the liquor that he had so carefully hidden.

Samuel P. Bates, Martial Deeds of Pennsylvania. (Philadelphia: T. H. Davis & Company, 1876). Charles Wills account, Gettysburg National Military Park

**

Early in the morning, Harry Heth's division of A. P. Hill's Corps broke camp at Cashtown, some seven miles west of Gettysburg. With the 13th Alabama in advance, they passed by the camps of Anderson's Division and headed out on the turnpike. Within about four miles of Gettysburg, they passed through a small village of a few brick houses (Seven Stars, Pennsylvania). About one-half mile past this village, the turnpike entered a thick woodland or swamp, where Archer's Brigade halted in the misty rain. Col. Birkett D. Fry quickly rode back to the color bearer and ordered him to uncase the colors, a sure sign that the regiment was about to engage the enemy. The Alabamans soon discovered a squad of dismounted Federal cavalry to their right in an old field, holding their horses. Fry ordered the regiment to file to the right into an apple orchard and to load their guns at will. Companies B,

...ith the 5th Alabama Battalion, were ordered forward ...nd them, the brigade formed into a long battle line ..."Forward, march!" was given and the Rebels slowly ...ine entered the swampy ground along Marsh Creek, a ...Battle of Gettysburg.

..."...attle of Gettysburg," The Confederate Veteran

**

...d's cavalry division halted Heth's advance long enough ...rive on McPherson's Ridge just west of Gettysburg. As ...l into Gettysburg on the morning of July 1, many were ...s the 153rd Pennsylvania approached the center of the ...ed to see a small girl passing out water in a tin dipper. ...ith an apron and bib decorated with the stars and stripes, ...ery shells that were bursting overhead. She continually ...fty-something father kept refilling with buckets of water ...am Kiefer took his refreshing turn at the dipper, he ...u." She calmly replied, "Oh, it's all right, I think" and

...the One Hundred and Fifty-third Regiment Regiment ...as Recruited in Northampton County, Pa. 1862-1863. (The

**

At the beginning of the battle as shots rang out and artillery thundered, many Gettysburg residents scurried about the streets, seeking shelter in fear that the town would soon be shelled. Military authorities soon ordered the people to stay off the streets, and many huddled together in cellars. A few hastily packed up and headed out of town, many passing by long columns of oncoming Federal troops. However on the northern outskirts of town, the situation was much different. According to young Anna Mary Young, "You could see the housetops covered with ladies, as well as gentlemen, watching the battle. Our family repaired to the attic, and from the windows we could see the movements of our troops." The true horrors of war had yet to become a reality for the citizens.

Anna Young account, Gettysburg National Military Park

**

For many of the approaching Union soldiers, thoughts that today would bring a battle were far from their minds. Col. Charles Wainwright, commanding the artillery of the

First Army Corps, breakfasted soon after sunrise, but "it rather promised then to be a quiet day for us. I was just finishing up my monthly return when the order came to move at once. We moved along very quietly without dreaming of a fight, and fully expecting to be comfortably in camp by noon. So confident of this was I that, for the first time, I threw my saddlebags into the wagon, and was thus left without my supply of chocolate and tobacco, without brush, comb, or clean handkerchief. My horse 'Billy' cast two shoes on the road. I had no hesitation on stopping at a farmhouse with one of my forges until they could be replaced and even sat there ten or fifteen minutes longer until a heavy shower was over." Wainwright, still not expecting a fight, soon rode to the head of his column and encountered Maj. Gen. Abner Doubleday. Their conversation was interrupted by the distant bursting of shells when a courier dashed up on a lathered horse and delivered a message ordering them to hasten to the front. Wainwright immediately complied. He would not get to enjoy his chocolate and tobacco again for days.

Charles Wainwright, A Diary of Battle, The Personal Journals of Colonel Charles S. Wainwright, 1861-1865, (New York: Harcourt, Brace & World, 1962).

**

As the 5th Alabama Battalion of Archer's Brigade advanced towards McPherson's Ridge, some of their skirmishers passed through a wheat field to a small cabin, expecting to use it for protection as they fired at some Yankees hiding in the woods beyond. Their attention was drawn to a fierce watchdog, whose loud and boisterous barking signaled his objection to the strangers trespassing on the property. As the skirmishers parlayed with the dog, his owner, a shoemaker, emerged from the cellar and ordered his dog to be quiet. He inquired, "What are you here for?" The Confederates informed him that a big battle was brewing and they were fixing to take a hand. "By whom?" the owner asked. "By Lee and the Yankees," answered the Rebels. They laughed when the shoemaker responded, "Tell Lee to hold on just a little until I get my cow in out of the pasture." Firing commenced soon afterwards, and the first casualty in the regiment was a little dog that had become the company's pet.

William F. Fulton, Jr., Family Record and War Reminiscences. (Livingston, AL: self-published, 1919).

**

The Union First Corps established a lengthy defensive line along McPherson's and Oak ridges from Fairfield Road to the Mummasburg Road. Pausing at a farm owned by Edward McPherson near the Chambersburg Pike, Cpl. Simon Hubler and his comrades of the 143rd Pennsylvania of Col. Roy Stone's brigade eagerly advanced to a deep well near the farmhouse, hoping to refresh themselves with cool water. An officer soon put an end to this by cutting the rope and allowing the bucket to fall into the recesses of the well. His goal was

40

to avoid the overheated men from indulging too freely in the cold water, and he needed to hustle them into battle line.

Undeterred, Pvt. John Shafer of I Company ran into the cellar and soon emerged toting a large crock of sour milk. He carried it into a nearby wagon shed to avoid detection, where he and several other soldiers took turns cupping their hands into the milk and lapping it down. As they were drinking, a Rebel shell suddenly tore a hole through the shed's roof. Shafer calmly remarked, "We had better hurry up because the ____ fools have our range, and might hurt somebody." The men quenched their thirst, then left the shed and passed through the barnyard, where another shell struck among the straw and manure, rolling for quite a distance before stopping. They hastened on to the turnpike and rejoined their regiment in the roadway.

Simon Hubler manuscript (August 12, 1912), used by written permission of Marcia Wilson. First published in the New York Times, June 29, 1913.

**

Twenty-two-year-old Andrew Crooks of Beaver County was a member of Company D of the 149th Pennsylvania in Stone's Brigade. As fighting intensified on McPherson's Ridge, he was helping carry an injured friend from the battlefield when he was severely wounded in the leg and both men fell in a heap. As the regiment's position became untenable due to overwhelming numbers of Confederates, Crooks' comrades left both of them lying on the battlefield. Suffering intense thirst from the open wound and from the heat of the day, Crooks and his friend lay with parched throats, their canteens being empty. The 149th was a new regiment, untested and untried, but equipped with new uniforms and accoutrements. As such, Crooks' canteen had a bright new cover. A passing Confederate was apparently attracted by the canteen, and swapped his old one for the shiny new one. Luckily for Crooks and his wounded friend, the Rebel canteen was full of good water.

Refreshed, he and his comrade were kept alive until they were removed from the battlefield to temporary hospitals. Unfortunately, his friend soon died of his wounds, but the gravely wounded Crooks was moved from hospital to hospital as he slowly regained his strength. On July 20, he was transported to the general hospital (Camp Letterman along the York Turnpike) and in September, he was finally removed to a hospital in Pittsburgh. He was later sent by train to Philadelphia to be fitted for a prosthetic leg. The train wrecked, killing several passengers, but again, Crooks had cheated death. He lived to be 93.

Gratiot County, Michigan, Historical Society

**

For area residents, the fighting brought personal loss and tragedy. Hundreds would suffer property damage, loss of livestock, and the destruction of vital crops and gardens. Some would suffer even more. West of Gettysburg between Fairfield Road and the

Chambersburg Pike was a large farm belonging to Baltimore merchant Emmanuel Harmon. In 1861, when talk of secession had divided loyalties in the city and created instability and danger, he had sent his 14-year-old daughter Amelia to live with his 53-year-old sister Susan Castle on the quiet farm west of meandering Willoughby Run. Amelia went to work assisting the town's venerable cobbler, John Burns.

Now, Confederate skirmishers and sharpshooters occupied the Harmon farm after driving off or killing Federals posted there in mid-morning. Amelia and her aunt had a bird's-eye view from the locked house's cupola. By early afternoon, the concealed Confederates were steadily picking off Union soldiers on nearby McPherson's Ridge. Annoyed by the persistent firing from the doors and windows of the house and barn, division commander James Wadsworth ordered the 80th New York to flush out the Rebels. In response, Col. Theodore Gates sent forward Company K, 30 men under Capt. Ambrose N. Baldwin. After a spirited contest, they seized the farm. Amelia and her aunt descended from the cupola and were ordered to take shelter in the dank cellar.

Soon, Confederate Gen. Henry Heth sent in his two remaining brigades and fighting escalated around the Harmon farm and the fields and woods south of the turnpike. Captain Baldwin and a reinforcement company held out for an hour. Finally, the 47th and 52nd North Carolina surged forward and surrounded the farm on three sides. The New Yorkers barely escaped, covered by the 8th Illinois Cavalry. Amelia and her aunt peered at the advancing Rebels from the narrow windows in the cellar. They saw smoke pouring from their barn and soon heard the heavy footsteps of men upstairs. Coming upstairs, they saw Rebels piling books, rugs, and pieces of furniture on a pile of burning newspapers on the floor. Unable to prevent the Confederates from firing their house, the pair of women fled the building. Running through fields teeming with enemy soldiers, they finally met a group of Confederate officers and newspapermen, who gave them sanctuary and food.

Amelia E. Harmon account, Gettysburg National Military Park

**

For hundreds of men, July 1 would be their last day on Earth. Some perished suddenly and quickly, their lifeless forms now lying in Pennsylvania farm fields and woodlots. For others came the grim realization that their fresh wounds were surely mortal. As the 6th Wisconsin charged a Confederate position in a railroad cut just north of the Chambersburg Pike, their ranks were thinned by Minié balls. Lt. Col Rufus Dawes, pushing his men forward, noted that one soldier had turned from the ranks and had staggered back beside him. Pulling open his woolen shirt to reveal a hole where a bullet had entered his chest, Corp. James Kelly of Company B gasped, "Colonel, won't you please write to my folks that I died as a soldier?"

Rufus R. Dawes, Service with the Sixth Wisconsin Volunteers. (Marietta, OH: E. R. Alderman, 1890)

Not everyone died a hero. North of Gettysburg, 15-year-old John Cabell Early, a nephew of General Early who served as one of his uncle's couriers, recorded one of the very first Confederate casualties as Early's division pressed forward towards a Union line near Rock Creek. "Soon orders were given for the advance. There was a rail fence in front of us, and the first man I saw killed was shot by a rail falling on the hammer of his own gun, the ball striking him on the chest and coming out at the back of his head." Somewhere in the South, a family would come to believe that their loved one had died a Gettysburg hero, slain by a hated Yankee, instead of being killed through a clumsy accident when he banged his cocked musket against a fence rail as he climbed over.

John Cabell Early, The Journal of the Military Service Institution, June, 1911.

**

In another case, sheer stupidity contributed to a man's mortifying wounding. The 13th Massachusetts had fallen back to Seminary Ridge and was enjoying a brief respite from the Confederate guns that had chased them from their first position. They took the respite to erect hasty works for added protection. Spent cannonballs could occasionally be seen rolling slowly along the earth, fired from the Rebel guns on distant Oak Hill. One of the officers happened to watch a Wisconsin soldier of the Iron Brigade learn painfully that these balls could still be lethal, even unexploded ones. The infantryman, "with great glee," put out a heel to stop one such ball that was rolling toward him, supposing it to be the easiest thing in the world to do. Those around him who sensed what he was planning to do screamed out their warnings, but it was too late. The ball, traveling much faster than the unfortunate soldier knew, had his leg ripped off by the impact of the collision. The poor fellow, in shock and disbelief as well as shame, "cried like a child" to think that he had lost his leg in such an undignified manner, when, as he said, he would have gladly lost it in action. He lived, but it was pitiable to see his grief as he exclaimed, "I shall always be ashamed to say how I lost it."

Charles E. Davis, Jr., Three Years in the Army. The Story of the Thirteenth Massachusetts Volunteers from July 16, 1861, to August 1, 1864" (Boston: Estes and Lauriat, 1894).

**

On the morning of July 1, the 45th New York, a regiment with a large percentage of recent German immigrants, was camped along the Emmitsburg Road in northern Maryland when news came that a battle was beginning near Gettysburg. Lt. Col. Adolphus Dobke moved his regiment at the double quick northward on the gravel road. Arriving in Gettysburg, they were ordered to take a position northwest of town near the Mummasburg Road. After driving Confederate snipers out of the Hagy orchard, four companies of the 45th advanced on an enemy position astride the McLean farm at the foot of Oak Hill. Supported by accurate artillery fire from fellow German Capt. Hubert Dilger's Ohio battery, the New Yorkers managed to drive the 5th Alabama from the farm. Surrounding the large red wooden barn, they took several prisoners. One of the dejected Rebels, a man named Schwarz, asked whether his brother, who belonged to Company B of the 45th, was among the captors. By coincidence, Companies A and B had taken most of the prisoners in the barn. The Confederate soon recognized his brother in the barnyard and they warmly embraced, not having seen each other since they had left Germany many years before. In a sad twist of irony, the Yankee brother, Cpl. Rudolph Schwarz, was killed not long afterward on the front lines while his Rebel brother was being marched to the rear as a prisoner of war.

Final Report on the Battlefield of Gettysburg (New York at Gettysburg). New York Monuments Commission for the Battlefields of Gettysburg and Chattanooga. (Albany, NY: J.B. Lyon Company, 1902).

**

Posted on a knoll north of Gettysburg along the Harrisburg Road, Battery G, 4th U.S. Light Artillery blazed away at a battalion of Confederate guns less than a mile to the northeast. Soon, the battery was also under fire from Oak Hill to the west. The air was thick with red-hot shell fragments, which sprayed death and injury with each burst. In command of the outnumbered Union battery was Lt. Bayard Wilkeson, the 19-year-old son of a newspaperman. His grandfather had been a founder of Buffalo and a wealthy judge and businessman who lived next door to Millard Fillmore, a President of the United States. A long way from the comforts of home, young Wilkeson was struck by a shell which nearly severed his right leg below the knee. He coolly formed a tourniquet with his belt, applied pressure to the leg and cut off the dangling remnant with his pocket knife. He was carried to the rear and laid in the Adams County Almshouse (the regional poorhouse).

When the Rebels overwhelmed the exposed position, the corps withdrew to Gettysburg, leaving the stricken Wilkeson and hundreds of other wounded men behind for the enemy. Late that evening, New York Times correspondent Samuel Wilkeson reached Meade's headquarters, where he learned that his son had been severely wounded and apparently captured. Days later when the Confederates had departed Gettysburg, the reporter was able to recover his son's body. He telegraphed his article to his editor, then mournfully collected the remains of Bayard and accompanied them home to Buffalo for his funeral and burial.

Files of the Gettysburg National Military Park; Ben Maryniak article on the Gettysburg Discussion Group

**

Not long after Wilkeson's wounding, Brig. Gen. John Gordon's Georgia brigade tangled with Francis Barlow's Eleventh Corps division along the same knoll. After a severe fight, the Yankees retreated and reformed in the rear of the Almshouse. A large number of frightened or injured Federal soldiers had taken refuge in a large 3-story brick barn between the lines. Gordon halted his brigade about 250 yards from this imposing barn. A call was made for volunteers to serve as skirmishers, as the position was dangerous, requiring soldiers with steady nerves and clear heads. Six men from Company H of the 38th Georgia (J. E. "Jep" Campbell, Green Seymore, William Kirby, John King, Jasper Harbin and Phil W. Alexander) stepped forward and announced their readiness to undertake the dangerous mission. They were ordered to advance to the barn and seize all the Yankees who wished to surrender. Under cover from their four comrades, Campbell and Kirby slowly worked their way to the barn and cautiously entered its door. They were surprised to find the building completely filled with Union soldiers, and they were sorely outnumbered.

Fearlessly, Private Kirby began to curse and abuse the Yankees with every insult he could think of. The quick-thinking Campbell decided on a different and more conciliatory policy, explaining to the enemy soldiers that Kirby was drunk and not responsible for what he said. He called on them to surrender, stating that the barn was now surrounded by large numbers of Confederates, and the building would be riddled by shells unless they gave themselves up. The Federals, badly demoralized by their earlier defeat and retreat, believed Campbell and consented to lay down their arms and surrender. So as to not betray the fact that there were in fact only two Confederates, Campbell made his prisoners march from the rear door of the barn by pairs, laying down their arms as they did so. In all, Gordon's brigade captured nearly 280 Federal soldiers near the Almshouse complex, a number of which were secured by Campbell's clever ruse.

Elberton (Georgia) Star, February 2, 1889

**

By mid-afternoon, the Confederates had more troops on the field than the Federals, and the weight of numbers and the exhaustion of the battered Union regiments began to tell. Both the First and Eleventh Army Corps began to withdraw through the streets of Gettysburg, and confusion reigned as soldiers and artillerists struggled to find their way to the rallying point on Cemetery Hill. In several cases, regimental discipline disappeared and knots of men worked their way to safety. Thousands were cut off and captured, however, as the Confederates closely pursued. The Richmond Howitzers unlimbered into battery along the old Harrisburg Road on Gettysburg's northern outskirts and prepared to sweep the streets in case of a sudden Yankee counterattack.

Artilleryman Robert Stiles noted that a solitary Confederate rider was passing by the battery, heading into town. Chubby 16-year-old George Greer, General Early's clerk and a particular favorite of "Old Jube," ignored Stiles' shouts of warning and disappeared into the smoke and dust in front of the battery. Soon, Stiles noted a cloud of blue-coats running down the street toward the guns. He was preparing to open fire when he noted little Greer, leaning forward over the neck of his horse, towering over the Federal foot soldiers. With violent gestures and in tones not gentle, the youth commanded the "blue devils" to double quick to the rear of one of the artillery pieces. The clerk had captured over fifty Yankees, who had thrown away their arms and were cowering in the streets and alleys when a quick thinking Greer rounded them up.

Robert Stiles, Four Years Under Marse Robert (New York/Washington: The Neale Publishing Company, 1904).

**

Surrender was not on the minds of many men, who desperately tried to avoid captivity. However, it was the destiny for thousands of Federals that afternoon. As the line of the First Army Corps along Oak Ridge began to crumble under repeated assaults, Brig. Gen. John Robinson knew he had to sacrifice some of his regiments in order to save what was left of his division. He sent an aide to instruct the commander of the 16th Maine to move forward to the Mummasburg Road. Soon, he rode over to Col. Charles W. Tilden and personally reiterated the order. A doubtful Tilden emphasized the strength of the enemy and expressed the opinion that it would be impossible to hold the position. Robinson very emphatically retorted, "Take that position and hold it at any cost." "You know what that means," replied Tilden as he turned and reluctantly ordered his regiment to about face and move forward. The men in ranks knew they were the sacrifice, and death, injury or captivity awaited many.

As quietly and orderly as if on parade, the regiment stoically moved forward and assumed the designated position. With less than 300 men, they were expected to delay several divisions of the enemy. Yet, they did so until the majority of their division had been safely withdrawn. Realizing that further fighting was useless, Colonel Tilden heard a call from the Rebels to surrender. He plunged his sword into the ground as far as he could and broke it off at the hilt rather than present it to his captor. Nearby, a Confederate officer tried to grasp the regiment's colors, but the men closed ranks and protected them long enough for the color bearer to break the staff and tear the flag into little pieces, which were concealed among the surviving soldiers and officers, who then laid down their arms. Out of 275 combatants in the 16th Maine, 11 were killed, 62 wounded, and 159 captured. Only 39 men and 4 officers escaped to Cemetery Hill.

Lt. Francis Wiggin, Sixteenth Maine Regiment at Gettysburg, War Papers, Maine MOLLUS, Volume 4, December 7, 1910.

**

The Iron Brigade reluctantly marched away from Seminary Ridge, having been ordered to "keep your men together" according to Col. Rufus Dawes of the 6th Wisconsin. When his regiment crossed the street extending through Gettysburg from the college to Cemetery Hill (Baltimore Street), they were now facing the enemy and turned their course toward the Cemetery Hill, although then unconscious of this fact. The first cross street was swept by Confederate musketry fire. There was a close board fence, enclosing a barnyard, on the opposite side of the street. A board or two missing from the fence made what the soldiers called a "hog hole." Instructing his regiment to follow in single file on the run, Dawes took a flag, raced across the street and jumped through the narrow opening. His officers and men followed rapidly. Taking position at the fence, when any man obstructed the passage-way through it, Dawes jerked him away without ceremony or apology, the object being to keep the track clear for those yet to come. Two men were shot in this street crossing. The regiment reformed in the sheltered barnyard, and then marched back again to Baltimore Street and thence ascended Cemetery Hill to safety.

Rufus R. Dawes, "With the Sixth Wisconsin at Gettysburg," Sketches of War History, Ohio MOLLUS, Volume 3

**

The retreating Yankees sought shelter wherever they could find it. As Cpl. Simon Hubler and some comrades in Company I of the 143rd Pennsylvania hastened through the streets in the western side of Gettysburg, they noted a large group of soldiers hiding behind a heaping mound of oyster shells. Rebel Minié balls were repeatedly striking these shells with a distinct zipping sound. Hubler hurried by the pile, remarking to the hidden soldiers that they had better be careful or they might be captured by the pursuing Rebels. He never found out if these men were indeed taken prisoner, or if they had made their escape to Cemetery Hill in the confusion.

Simon Hubler manuscript (August 12, 1912), used by written permission of Marcia Wilson. First published in the New York Times, June 29, 1913.

**

Col. Aldolphus Dobke led the 45th New York back towards Gettysburg from their position along the Mummasburg Road. As they reached the town square, a sudden panic arose in the regiment just in front of them. Not wanting his regiment to become mixed up in the confusion, Dobke turned the 45th down another street, marching two blocks before turning again toward Cemetery Hill. About the middle of the block, when the column came under the enemy's infantry fire, the men quickly headed into an alley leading in the general direction they needed to go. Unfortunately, this alley led into a spacious yard surrounded by large buildings. The only way to pass out of this yard was by a very narrow doorway, but Confederate sharpshooters had already piled a barricade of dead Union soldiers in the street just in front of this door. About 100 New Yorkers managed to extricate themselves from this death trap, running through a gauntlet of fire before arriving safely at the hilltop graveyard. The rest of the men were captured.

The War of the Rebellion: A Compilation of the Official Records of the Union and Confederate Armies, 70 volumes in 4 series. Washington, D.C.: United States Government Printing Office, 1880-1901.

**

In some cases, Federal soldiers managed to escape becoming prisoners of war by hiding out with Gettysburg residents. Men of all ranks tried to avoid detection as Confederate patrols scoured the borough. German-born Brig. Gen. Alexander Schimmelfennig had his horse shot and killed as he rode through town. As he was about to be cut off by a band of Rebels, he leaped over a fence and took cover behind a shed in the backyard of the Garlach property on Baltimore Street. The next day, Anna Garlach and her mother learned of their unexpected guest's presence. Mrs. Garlach made a pretense of carrying a bucket to be emptied into the swill barrel. Instead, the bucket contained water and a piece of bread, which she furtively gave to the hidden officer. Afraid that she had been spotted in her subterfuge, she did not repeat her act of kindness. When the Confederates finally withdrew from town on July 4, a cold, hungry and exceedingly thirsty Schimmelfennig emerged from the old wooden outbuilding, his body stiff from being cramped into such a small space where he dared not stand erect.

Anna Garlach account, Gettysburg National Military Park

**

The frantic retreat from the fields and ridges west and north of Gettysburg created chaos at times as regimental discipline broke down. The houses and shops of Gettysburg overflowed with wounded from the day's battles, and the surgeons and hospital stewards faced a grim choice – abandon their wounded and join the withdrawal to presumed safety, or stay with the injured and take their chances of becoming prisoners of war. In the late afternoon, fleeing men from the Eleventh Corps raced past a temporary hospital headed by Dr. Jacob Ebersole, surgeon of the 19th Indiana of the First Corps' famed Iron Brigade. His hospital steward, in great alarm and perturbation, hastily came to Ebersole and inquired, "Shall I go to the front or stay with you?" The steward, being an enlisted man, greatly feared being taken captive and landing in Andersonville or some other prison.

Ebersole calmly replied, "Do as you think best, but whatever you do, act quickly." The steward snatched up his hat and coat and hastened downstairs to the street. Ebersole called out, "Take my horse!" as that was the only sure way to escape. Going to the window to see what would happen, Ebersole saw his horse fastened to the fence across the street, with great saddlebags and blankets, all his army treasures strapped upon him. At that moment, just before the steward could reach the horse, one of the fleeing soldiers leaped into the saddle, and both rider and horse disappeared in an instant with the steward racing behind on foot. As the shadows lengthened, the doctor watched in shock from the upper floor windows, watching the remaining lines being repulsed and the boys in blue falling back in utter confusion. Soon, the enemy enveloped the town from that side, sweeping past the hospital and completely filling the streets.

Ebersole remained with his wounded patients during the Rebel occupation. To his relief, when they withdrew on July 4, they did not take him prisoner with them, but left him in the house. On Sunday, Ebersole to his astonishment discovered that his stolen horse, with all his trappings still on his back, was safely housed with those of his brigade, awaiting the doctor's return to the lines. He remained at the hospital a fortnight, working day and night, until he was ordered to rejoin his regiment, which was in Virginia pursuing Lee.

Jacob Ebersole, M.D., "Incidents of Field Hospital Life With the Army of the Potomac," Sketches of War History, Ohio MOLLUS.

**

While fighting raged at Gettysburg on July 1, tens of thousands of troops on both sides were still en route to the crossroads town. The 16th Pennsylvania Cavalry, a part of J. Irvin Gregg's division, rode through the countryside between Westminster, Maryland and Hanover, Pennsylvania. Pvt. Samuel Cormany of Chambersburg ate a "fine chicken breakfast and a feast of other good things." With his appetite sated, he had time to observe the lush, rich farmland along the hot and dusty roads. In particular, he observed that the region had "such fine water." The inhabitants, whom he described as "Old Style People," including many Dunkers, were quite pleased to see the Union cavalrymen and fed them all along their route. They regaled the soldiers with stories of how meanly they had been treated by the Confederates who had passed that way the previous day (Stuart's Cavalry). Several Rebels had blackmailed the farmers, demanding money to exempt their horses from capture and to insure that their barns and houses were not burned. One old farmer had paid $100 to exempt his two horses, another paid $23 to keep his horse. Still another farmer had paid $100 to save his barn from the torch. An astonished Cormany recorded in his diary that evening "this hideous thing was quite common."

Samuel Cormany diary, July 1, 1863, Franklin County Historical Society

**

By late afternoon, Lee's troops again occupied Gettysburg, but under much different circumstances than Jubal Early's stay the previous week. Fences were destroyed, gardens trampled, bullet holes pockmarked several homes, and bodies wearing blue and gray lay in the streets and yards. As the firing ceased and the residents learned that the Confederates meant them no harm, the residents began emerging to witness the carnage, and in many cases, to render whatever assistance they could to hundreds of wounded soldiers. Bedrooms, living rooms, parlors, barns, outbuildings, and porches became temporary hospitals as the citizens, in some cases aided by military doctors, began the unenviable task of comforting the injured.

Young Albertus McCreary later wrote that when the Rebels reached his house, five of them suddenly opened the cellar door and jumped down into the family huddled there. Some of the women cried, others were numb with fear. Mr. McCreary stepped forward and asked the Rebels what they wanted, and begged that his family not be harmed. The Rebels replied that they were looking for Union soldiers. Despite McCreary's insistence that there were none present, the Rebels decided to search the house. They eventually rounded up thirteen frightened Federals; some rooted from under beds and in closets and one pried out from his hiding place under a piano. Armed Confederates shepherded them into the McCreary's dining room where officers took down the names of the prisoners. Soon, both sides were laughing and chatting like old friends, and the family could return to their upstairs without fear.

Albertus McCreary, "Gettysburg: A Boy's Experience of the Battle," McClure's Magazine, Volume 33 (July 1909)

**

Concurrent with the fighting at Gettysburg on July 1, Gen. J.E.B. Stuart's cavalrymen wearily rode through York County, Pennsylvania, in a futile attempt to connect with Lee's army. They had missed rendezvousing with Early's division at York, and were now headed northwest to Carlisle in hope of finding Ewell. The region contained a curious mixture of ardent Unionists, ambivalent German farmers who mostly just wanted to be left alone, and "Copperheads" (Confederate sympathizers). An officer in Capt. James Breathed's Virginia horse artillery battery, Lt. F. Halsey Wigfall, wrote to his sister: "You should have seen the Dutch people in York Co. turning out with water and milk and bread and butter and 'apple butter' for the 'ragged rebels.' I was quite surprised at the tone of feeling in that part of the State. In two or three instances I found people who seemed really glad to see us and at scores of houses they had refreshments at the door for the soldiers. The people generally seemed not to know exactly what to expect and I don't think would have been at all astonished if every building had been set on fire by us as we reached it, nor would a great many have been surprised if we had concluded the business by massacring the women and children!"

Eighteen-year-old Wigfall continued, "I stopped at a house in Petersburg, Adams Co., Penn. and almost the first question addressed me by the daughter of the house, a girl of eighteen or twenty and a perfect Yankee, was whether our men would molest the women! I told her not, and she seemed to feel considerably reassured. It was this same girl who told me in all seriousness that she had heard and believed it, that the Southern women all wore revolvers."

Mrs. D. Giraud Wright, A Southern Girl in '61: The War-Time Memories of a Confederate Senator's Daughter. (New York: Doubleday, Page & Company, 1905).

**

Tens of thousands of men still marched on the hot, dusty roads towards Gettysburg on July 1 as commanders hastened up the rest of the two armies. One regiment of Massachusetts men in the Twelfth Corps was wearily hiking up the Emmitsburg Road. As they passed through one small village, a local woman passed among the grimy and dust-laden soldiers "with evident delight," shaking hands and offering greetings and pleasantries. Soon, an unfurled American flag passed by. In great disgust, she spit out, "I thought you were Rebs." She quickly turned around and stalked off.

**

In the confusion of the long day at Gettysburg, many Union regiments found that their supply wagons were not nearby, and in several cases, the famished men did not have fresh provisions. As the predominantly Irish 9th Massachusetts found shelter and laid down for the evening, one infantryman, more hungry and wide awake than the rest, rose and began scrounging for food. He approached a dead soldier, by whose side was a well-filled haversack. Kneeling down by the body, he opened the haversack and saw, revealed by the bright moonlight, a "goodly feast of flour rolls, looking temptingly brown and nice." Apparently, the poor fallen soldier had purchased them on the march, but had not had time to eat before he was engaged in his last fight. One by one, the sleepless soldier transferred the rolls to his own haversack before rising to return to the regiment.

He moved about two paces and suddenly stopped to the astonishment of a couple of onlookers. Pausing a moment in seeming meditation, he turned back to where the dead soldier was lying, his pale face revealed by the moonlight. Once again kneeling gently down by his side, one by one he took the rolls from his haversack and replaced them in their original place. Carefully drawing a blanket over the face of the dead man, he slowly moved away, too conscientious to despoil the dead of his food, although he was very hungry.

Michael H. Macnamara, The Irish Ninth Massachusetts in Bivouac and Battle. (Boston: Lee and Shepard, 1867).

**

Meanwhile in the Rebel occupied town, soldiers and civilians warily eyed each other. Most weary Confederates simply laid down wherever they could to seek a few hours of shut-eye. However, schoolteacher Sallie Broadhead and her husband could not sleep with the anxiety of the night. They watched as Rebels robbed the house across the street, hastily abandoned when the owners had fled. "They went from the garret to the cellar, and, loading up the plunder in a large four-horse wagon, drove it off. I expected every minute that they would burst into our door, but they did not come near us."

Sarah Broadhead account, Gettysburg National Military Park

**

A few Confederate soldiers, weary of warfare, took advantage of the confusion of the day to desert the army. Northeast of Gettysburg on their rural hilltop farm, the Bayly family was awakened sometime after midnight by loud knocking at their front door. Harriet Bayly asked her 13-year-old son Billy to follow her downstairs. Opening the door, they found a "little fellow in a gray uniform," hardly taller than Billy and only a couple of years older. The excited Rebel mentioned that he had been in the battle, his company had been cut to pieces, he was from North Carolina, was tired of the fighting, and never wanted to see another battle. Would the family conceal him until the battle was over? A sympathetic Mrs. Bayly, undoubtedly touched by this young soldier who wasn't much different than her own son, whisked him into the house and gave him a set of civilian clothing. She led him to the garret, where the featherbeds were stored for the summer, and told him to select a bed and get some sleep. When Lee retreated on July 4, the lad stayed behind and became a permanent resident of Adams County, his days in the Confederate army now only a memory.

William Hamilton Bayly account, Gettysburg National Military Park.

**

Rumors remained rampant among the troops at Gettysburg and those still on the march. Shortly before midnight, the 16th Michigan Infantry passed through the sleepy village of McSherrystown near the border between York and Adams counties in southern Pennsylvania. Somehow, a rumor began spreading that Governor Curtin and President Lincoln had spent the day conferring and working behind the scenes, and now Maj. Gen. George B. McClellan had been reinstated at the head of the Army of the Potomac and was rushing to rejoin the command. Cheering began at the head of the mile-long column and quickly word spread through the ranks – Little Mac was indeed back! Cheer after cheer rent the night air.

According to Lt. Ziba Graham, wearied boys, who but a short time before had been dejected, now were delirious with joy. Old veterans openly cried with exhilaration and relief, and on the moonlit night, kepis and caps were thrown up into the air in celebration of the welcomed news. Old men and women from the village emerged to cheer, cry, and minister to the passing troops. According to Graham, "Truly, it was a sight never to be forgotten." Many of the men would enter combat on the morrow still believing that McClellan was on the scene. It later turned out that it was New Jersey's governor, Joel Parker, who was clamoring for McClellan, but Washington had turned deaf ears to the proposal. The general would never return to his army, and would be disappointed a year later when the troops solidly supported Lincoln's bid for re-election.

Ziba B. Graham, "On to Gettysburg: Ten Days from My Diary," War Papers, Michigan MOLLUS, Volume 1

Chapter 3

The Battle of Gettysburg
Thursday, July 2, 1863

As daybreak came, the citizens of the Gettysburg region knew they were in for a hard time, as the Confederates still occupied the town and controlled access to most roads leading to the borough. Neither army showed any signs of withdrawing. A 23-year-old farmer and shoemaker, Emmanuel G. Trostle, lived along the Emmitsburg Road three miles south of Gettysburg with his wife Mary and infant son Harry. A Confederate colonel rode up to the farmhouse one evening and advised him to take his family and leave the place, as their lives would be endangered. Although young, Trostle was crippled at the time and could only walk with the aid of a staff and crutch. He informed the Rebel officer that he could not pass through the picket lines on his own. The colonel personally escorted him through the lines.

However, the next morning, Trostle became uneasy about his household goods and, accompanied by a friend, started back down Emmitsburg Road to return to the abandoned house. However, Confederate pickets arrested them and took them to their lines. Trostle expected to be paroled, but as firing resumed in the late afternoon, the paperwork could not be filled out. When the Rebels withdrew, they took Trostle and other civilians with them. Despite his handicap, he was forced to accompany them 175 miles to Staunton, Virginia, painfully walking for six days, the final three without any food to eat. He was detained in a variety of prison camps in Richmond and in Salisbury, North Carolina for 22 months. He had been reported as being killed, but his wife always held out hope of seeing him alive again. After his eventual release, Trostle returned to Gettysburg, amazingly in better health than previous to his captivity. After the war, he briefly moved to Illinois, before returning to Gettysburg, where he eventually bought a 52-acre farm and raised three children.

History of Cumberland and Adams Counties, Pennsylvania (Chicago: Warner, Beers & Co., 1886).

**

Prior to the Confederate invasion, a number of the men and older boys from the Gettysburg region had taken livestock and family valuables to safety – at times hiding in the woods, or transporting them to Harrisburg, York, or to Lancaster County. Many men had not yet returned to town. Those that had stayed now had new concerns as the Confederates occupied town. Many huddled in basements with their families. Some worked feverishly to assist the doctors and stewards comfort the wounded. In other cases, the men were more concerned with their personal safety.

Henry Garlach owned an old-fashioned, two-story brick building close to the sidewalk on South Baltimore Street, the main thoroughfare leading from town to the scene of the second and third days' battles and connecting with the Emmitsburg Road. Garlach, a man about forty-five years of age, was a cabinetmaker by trade, but also engaged in the manufacture of coffins and caskets, which unfortunately now offered the promise of considerable immediate work. Garlach's family consisted of his wife, a few years younger than himself, two daughters, one aged eighteen and the other quite small, and two sons, one of the latter an infant but a few months old. "During the occupancy of the town by the enemy, the father fled to the woods for fear of being impressed into service, while the mother and children remained in the cellar of the house for safety from exploding shells and stray bullets."

Fear of serving in the Rebel army had overwhelmed Garlach to the point where he abandoned his family. Ironically, his backyard shed / pigpen housed a hidden Federal general during the same time frame that Garlach was hiding in the woods. His home was filled with wounded Union soldiers, including Lt. Charles Roberts of the 17th Maine, who had lost an arm. The front hall being very narrow and small, Roberts was admitted through a window and a comfortable bed made in the parlor near the windows overlooking the street. He would stay in the house for nearly 5 weeks before being transferred to his home in Maine.

Charles W. Roberts, "At Gettysburg in 1863 and 1888," War Papers, Maine MOLLUS, Volume 1, paper read December 1888.

**

For some already in the Confederate army who had grown tired of war, the confusion at Gettysburg provided an opportunity to desert. Lt. Jeremiah Hoffman of the 142nd Pennsylvania, a wounded prisoner held in the Lutheran Seminary, noted one of his captors was a "long, lank, ignorant North Carolina mountaineer," a reluctant soldier who "was in continual fear of everybody and everything." He longed to desert, but was deathly afraid of the Pennsylvania Dutch, "a terrible people, who would be apt to kill him upon sight." Hoffman reassured the Rebel that the Dutch were kind-hearted, quiet and honest people, who were mostly concerned with their farms. Later, he learned that the Tar Heel was now hiding in the lower part of the seminary building and was indeed planning to steal off into the countryside.

Michael A. Dreese, "Ordeal in the Lutheran Theological Seminary: The Recollections of First Lt. Jeremiah Hoffman, 142nd Pennsylvania Volunteers," The Gettysburg Magazine, Number 23, July 2000.

Throughout much of the morning and early afternoon, the streets in southern Gettysburg were very dangerous places, as Union soldiers near Cemetery Hill exchanged fire with Confederate sharpshooters hidden in buildings and behind fences and trees. Marksmen, located in the steeple of the German Reformed Church on the southeastern part of the borough, were particularly annoying. They wounded several men and two officers, Lts. Nicholas Sahm and Christian Stock, of Weidrich's Battery I, 1st New York Artillery, which was positioned on the slopes of East Cemetery Hill. They also killed some of the battery's horses. The gunner of the third piece, notwithstanding orders not to fire into the town, loaded his gun with a shell and fired it at the steeple. It missed, but had the desired effect of silencing the enemy rifles.

Final Report on the Battlefield of Gettysburg (New York at Gettysburg) by the New York Monuments Commission for the Battlefields of Gettysburg and Chattanooga. (Albany, NY: J.B. Lyon Company, 1902).

**

Most of the battlefield was quite peaceful throughout the morning, with only occasional sniping except around the town itself. Warren Goss, a Union soldier on Cemetery Ridge, recorded his impressions of the peaceful pastoral scene on this bright clear day. "By ten o'clock the threatening skies vanished and the green meadows were bathed in sunlight, with here and there the shadow of transient clouds flitting across the sunlit valley and hills. Cattle were grazing in the fields below; the shrill crowing of the chanticleer was heard from neighboring farmyards; tame pigeons cooed on the hillside, and birds sang among the trees… On our right was the cemetery with its white monuments, among which shone the burnished brass pieces of artillery and the glittering bayonets of the infantry. Beyond this were seen the spires of the town, while farther to the right and rear was Culp's Hill. Running across our front, obliquely, was the Emmitsburg Road, while farther beyond was Seminary Ridge, on which the enemy was posted. On our left, over a mile distant, rose the sugar-loaf summits of the Round Tops." The idyllic scene would give way to carnage and chaos in the late afternoon, but for now, the men watched the distant puffs of white smoke that marked the scattered exchanges of gunfire from the forward skirmishers.

Warren Lee Goss, Recollections of a Private. (New York: Thomas Y. Crowell & Co., 1890).

**

At dawn, most of Daniel Sickles' Third Army Corps had been in line of battle, stretching out southward from Cemetery Ridge. General Sickles did not like the position, fearing that the Confederates could create havoc if they placed guns along the Emmitsburg Road on high ground near a sprawling peach orchard. He began developing plans to move his entire corps forward to occupy and protect this ground. In the meantime, many of his soldiers had enjoyed very little to eat and were quite hungry. By 3:00 p.m., the men of Col. Elijah Walker's 4th Maine had not eaten a meal since the previous day's lunch, having subsisted on water along with whatever they could scrounge in their meager haversacks. With no sign of any impending Confederate activity, Walker decided to allow his men a respite. Fires were kindled, a heifer was found nearby and slaughtered, coffee was steeped and beef impaled on sticks was warmed over the blaze. The soldiers brewed coffee and consumed the very rare and thoroughly smoked meat, sprinkling it with salt, a condiment that every soldier carried in his pocket. The beef may have been undercooked, but to the famished men, it tasted like heaven. Unknown to many of them, they too would be slaughtered that afternoon before the food even had time to be digested. The regiment's flag would be pierced by thirty-two bullets and two shell fragments, attesting to the enemy firepower that was poured into the boys from Maine.

Regimental Dedication of the 4th Maine Infantry Monument, October 10, 1888, Speech of Colonel Elijah Walker (GNMP)

**

Alexander Givin of the 114th Pennsylvania, a red-trousered Zouave regiment in line near the Peach Orchard, gave one of his men 10 cents to buy him some flour at the nearby Trostle house. The soldier returned with word that they were completely sold out of everything. However, Givin did procure some flour by other means and soon had a fire built. He hastily made a paste of flour and water, which he eagerly devoured to sate his appetite. One of his tentmates, Sgt. Joseph DeHaven also made a similar cup of the sticky goo, but was unable to enjoy it as the Confederates emerged from the woods on a nearby ridge and fighting began in earnest. DeHaven had missed his final meal. He, Givin and several others had a custom of meeting together each day to read a few verses of scripture, then one of the group would offer prayer. On the march to Gettysburg, they had put their heads together as they knelt on the ground and earnestly prayed. Rising, Sergeant DeHaven turned to his comrades and gravely said, "Boys, this is the last time we will pray together." His premonition proved true, as DeHaven was killed shortly after the Confederates attacked the Peach Orchard.

Memoirs of Alexander Wallace Givin, 114th Pennsylvania Volunteer Infantry.

**

Premonitions of impending death haunted many Civil War soldiers. In some cases, it was a desired fate. Lt. Henry A. L. French of the 12th New Hampshire Infantry had explored the West prior to the war. He returned home in 1860, secured a job and married. He joined the army in the summer of 1862, and shortly afterwards received word that his wife Sarah had successfully delivered a baby. He received a furlough and rushed home to visit his spouse and child. However, his joy soon turned to agony and depression, as Sarah died not long after Henry rejoined his regiment. On the long march to Gettysburg, the despondent French told his captain that he hoped to be killed in the next fight. On July 2, the 12th N.H. was hotly engaged along the Emmitsburg Road north of the Peach Orchard. An order came to "change front to the rear," a very hard thing to do while under fire without the men breaking ranks. While executing this maneuver, the lines wavered. Lieutenant French waved his sword and shouted, "Steady men, steady there!" Just then a Minié ball struck him in the head and passed through, killing him instantly. He was buried in an unmarked grave by the Confederates.

H. L. Robinson, History of Pittsfield, N. H. in the Rebellion (Pittsfield, NH: self published, 1893).

**

In one well-known instance, the person convinced of his own impending death was a brigade commander, a person of rank and authority who suspected his destiny and planned accordingly. On June 28, Col. Edward E. Cross, a 31-year-old native of New Hampshire, had led his brigade across Sugarloaf Mountain near Boonsboro, Maryland. His aide, 19-year-old Charles Hale, accompanied the commander, along with an officer from the 5th New Hampshire as they rode along the dusty road. After several hours of routine conversation regarding the regiment and military matters, the dialogue turned to the impending battle that was certain once the Army of the Potomac located and caught up to Lee's forces. Gravely, Cross remarked, "It will be my last battle," which shocked his companions. Hale, who had noted that Cross had seemed abstract or preoccupied for a few days, did not reply. Eventually, Cross continued, "Mr. Hale, I wish you to attend to my books and papers; that private box of mine in the headquarters wagon; you helped me re-pack it the other day. After the campaign is over, get it at once, dry the contents if damp, and then turn it over to my brother Richard." Hale's emotions turned to resentment, as he did not believe in premonitions and such demoralizing talk, especially from a ranking officer on the eve of battle. However, he kept his tongue in check.

The following day, Cross once again spoke of his future demise, this time in front of his entire staff after a long march of 30 miles. This time, Hale did not stay silent. He testily remarked about the foolishness of entertaining such ideas, mentioning that he did not believe in such things. Cross and Hale exchanged heated words, temporarily straining their once friendly relationship. However, on the evening of July 1 while camping at Uniontown, Maryland, Cross seemed his old self, jovial and positive in attitude. A relieved Hale assumed that the colonel had dismissed the subject from his mind. He was quite wrong.

As the brigade marched to the battlefield on July 2, Cross resumed his gloomy outlook. In a grave, firm manner, he intoned, "Mr. Hale, attend to that box of mine at the first opportunity." This brief remark convinced Hale that he was in dead earnest and still maintained a firm conviction of his impending fate. Shortly afterwards, Cross took the arm of one of his subordinate officers, Col. Boyd McKeen of the 81st Pennsylvania, and walked a short distance, heads bowed in earnest conversation. After walking a little ways they stopped, grasped hands a moment, then turned and walked back to where Hale and the brigade staff were standing. As they intently stared at their commander, Cross remarked, "Gentlemen, Colonel McKeen will command the one hundred and forty-eighth Pennsylvania today; before night he will probably be commanding the brigade."

In the early afternoon sunshine, the brigade waited for orders to advance. Colonel Cross impatiently paced back and forth in a quick nervous way, his hands clasped behind his back, a habit that was usual with him. Stopping near his watching aide, he reached into his inside pocket and drew a large new black silk handkerchief, which he folded over his lifted knee. Handing his hat to Hale, Cross quickly swathed his head with the cloth in turban fashion, tying the two ends behind before replacing his hat. His men had been amused on other battlefields when Cross had previously done the same thing with a bright red handkerchief. This time, especially after the peculiar circumstances of the past few days, the black handkerchief was appalling to the onlookers. Apparently not satisfied, he again took off his hat, saying, "Please tie it tighter Mr. Hale." With trembling hands, Hale picked at the knot. Cross impatiently ordered Hale to "draw it tighter still" until he was satisfied with the tautness.

By this time, the roar of battle could be clearly heard towards the right from the Peach Orchard, as well as to the rear near the Round Tops. Second Corps commander Winfield Hancock, a well-known major general and the veteran of many battles, coolly rode up from the left accompanied by his staff. He briefly reined his horse and intoned in a measured manner, "Colonel Cross this day will bring you a star." The colonel gravely shook his head as he calmly replied with no apparent emotion, "No general, this is my last battle." Hancock rode off, turning his attention to the direction of the Peach Orchard, where the battle was now raging at a white heat.

Soon, Cross's men were hotly engaged themselves near the Wheatfield. He stood among his battle line, barking out orders even as men dropped all around him. Soon, he walked into a patch of woods where the 148th Pennsylvania and the 5th New Hampshire were sorely pressed by the Confederates. Within five minutes, he had taken a bullet. By midnight that evening, true to his premonition, Edward Cross was indeed a dead man. His men could not help but ruefully recall his words, "I think the boys will miss me."

Major Charles A. Hale, With Colonel Cross in the Gettysburg Campaign. (GNMP files)

**

Among those killed at Gettysburg was a young Chinese man, known to his comrades as "John Tommy." He had entered the United States immediately after the war began and was induced to enlist in General Sickles' brigade, which was being recruited in New York City. He served in Captain Price's Company D of the 70th New York (the First Regiment of the "Excelsior Brigade" in the Third Corps). Although a mere lad, entirely ignorant of English, he soon became a favorite in the regiment through his intelligence, wit and honesty. In early 1862, he was taken prisoner during a reconnaissance mission on the Maryland shore of the Potomac River. He was brought before Confederate General John Magruder, who, surprised at his appearance and color, asked him if he was a mulatto, Indian, or what? When Tommy told him he was from China, Magruder was very much amused and asked him how much he would take to join the Confederate army. "Not unless you would make me a brigadier general," said Tommy, to the great delight of the Secesh officers, who treated him very kindly and forwarded him on to Fredericksburg. There, Tommy became a great amusement and his picture was published in the local newspapers. Subsequently he was sent to Libby Prison in Richmond, where he rejoined his captain, Benjamin Price, who had been taken prisoner at Williamsburg.

After his parole Tommy had returned to New York City, attending his sick and wounded comrades. He was the kindest of nurses, and spent his little means in providing delicacies for his sick fellow soldiers. Rejoining the regiment on active duty, he fought in the subsequent engagements at Fredericksburg, Chancellorsville, and Gettysburg, where he was struck by a shell which tore off both legs at the thighs, causing him to quickly bleed to death. The company went into the action with twenty-eight men, and lost twenty in killed and wounded. John Tommy was one of the very few Chinese-born men to serve in the Army of the Potomac, and as far as is known, the only one who perished at Gettysburg.

Files of the New York State Military Museum, Saratoga Springs, NY.

**

The 2nd New Hampshire was also part of Sickles' Third Corps. When the corps advanced to the Peach Orchard, the regiment was assigned the unenviable duty of supporting a battery stationed near the Emmitsburg Road. The position was precarious, exposed to a persistent crossfire of Confederate artillery and Minié balls. One incident showed the coolness of the Yankee boys, and also their enduring love for the "Almighty Dollar." As the fighting intensified, one soldier remembered a small debt owed him by one of his comrades, and, thinking of the uncertainty of life under such circumstances, decided to collect the money while he and the debtor still had time. During the fiercest of the contest, when the air was full of bursting shells and whistling bullets, he left his place in the ranks and hastened to the center of the line where the colors were waving. There, his comrade was actively engaged in protecting the flag of his country and sustaining the honor of the Old Granite State. As balls whizzed by, the first soldier apologized for the intrusion, said he might not have another opportunity to meet him, and that he would consider it a great favor if he would pay the debt. The debtor coolly reached into his purse and repaid his obligation, even as Confederate fire poured into the Union position. Having received his due payment, the satisfied soldier coolly returned to his place in the ranks, with the evident satisfaction of one who had done his duty to himself, his country, and all mankind, not to mention his pocketbook. Both men survived the battle without injury, although the regiment lost 193 officers and men from the 380 taken into the Peach Orchard.

Farmington Weekly Courier, February 5, 1864, Rochester, NH.

Even in the midst of combat, thievery was on the mind of some soldiers. In one case, it cost a man his life. During the terrific struggle along the Emmitsburg Road, Gen. Andrew Humphreys and his aide, Capt. William H. Chester of the 74th New York, were well in front, a place not often frequented by division commanders per standard military protocol of the day. Some of Humphreys' men were, for the moment, slowly giving way. The captain turned to rally them, facing the general, when a Minié ball entered near his spine and passed out in front. He exclaimed, "I am struck." Humphreys passed his arm around his aide to support him from the field. At this instant, the general's horse was killed, and he was obliged to consign the wounded Chester to an orderly while he directed his attention elsewhere. Hardly had they moved to retreat when a shell plowed into the group, instantly killing the orderly and tearing off his horse's head. Soon afterwards, a Confederate approached the prostrated captain, who seemed to be dead, and began stealing his watch. Summoning sufficient strength, Chester killed the robber with his pistol. Briefly rallying, his comrades soon rescued him, finding on one side the faithful dead orderly, and on the other, the Rebel thief. The popular Chester was taken to the Third Corps hospital near Gettysburg, where he survived eight days before finally expiring. His remains were transported home to New York for interment in the family vault.

Files of the New York State Military Museum, Saratoga Springs, NY.

**

Although the primary fighting raged in the fields and hills surrounding Gettysburg, there remained considerable danger to the townspeople that had not fled the borough when the Confederates approached. The Rev. Mr. Jacob Ziegler and his family huddled in their cellar for three days as Minié balls whizzed through the air just outside their home. His eldest daughter Anna ignored the bullets that would claim her former schoolmate Virginia "Ginnie" Wade and hastily walked two blocks to obtain yeast to be used for baking bread for the Union soldiers still in the vicinity. Miraculously, she was unharmed and returned successfully with the yeast. After the battle, Anna helped clean the Catholic church that was near her parents' home. The church had been used as a temporary hospital for wounded soldiers.

East Berlin (PA) News Comet, October 17, 1930.

**

For the soldiers waiting to enter the growing combat, the suspense and stress was at times unbearable. The 118th Pennsylvania lay prone in a field near the Rose Woods east of the Emmitsburg Road. Suddenly a thoroughly frightened rabbit, flushed from the fields where Lafayette McLaws' Confederate division was advancing, rushed toward the position of the Pennsylvanians. With a bound, he leaped into the unsuspecting ranks and "plunged his cold, sharp claws firmly into the neck of a soldier who lay flat near the edge of the regiment." The infantryman leaped to his feet and loudly cried to his comrades that he was surely a dead man, as he had been shot and the ball had passed completely through his neck. The men beside him, who had witnessed the rabbit's inadvertent assault, roared with laughter. They finally told the distraught soldier that his attacker was merely a rabbit, and he sheepishly resumed his place. Confederate accounts also mention this scared rabbit, which had previously escaped several poorly aimed shots from Wofford's Georgians.

History of the 118th Pennsylvania Volunteers: Corn Exchange Regiment... (Philadelphia: J. L. Smith, 1905).

**

Not only the townspeople and soldiers sensed the excitement and danger as the battle lines ebbed and flowed and the roar of musketry and artillery filled the air. The wildlife and remaining farm animals and pets were also affected by the conflict. The 11th Massachusetts formed on a fence along the Emmitsburg Road, sending out skirmishers into the fields beyond the Peter Rogers house and barn. Just as the troops and guns to their left at the Peach Orchard began giving way, the men suddenly could see Rebels swarming to their front, advancing from the woods towards their position. Huddling in the field taking potshots at the oncoming Southerners, some of the skirmishers suddenly turned their attention to a new and more immediate danger, dispatching a threatening snake that rustled in the tall grass. They soon withdrew to the road to rejoin the main line, which was partially sheltered by the Rogers home. When the Confederates drew near, they unloosed a volley that riddled the frame house. According to Lt. Henry N. Blake, "A kitten, mewing piteously, ran from it, jumped upon the shoulders of one of the men and remained there a few minutes during the fight."

Henry N. Blake, Three Years in the Army of the Potomac (Boston: Lee and Shepard, 1865).

**

The overall commander of the Army of the Potomac's artillery, Henry J. Hunt, spent much of July 2 on the southern portion of the battlefield, helping place batteries and troops. He had previously sent off his small staff with messages and now he was alone, an awkward thing for a general who had to keep up communications with every part of a battlefield and with the general-in-chief, George G. Meade. Climbing to the summit of Houck's Ridge near Devil's Den, Hunt found that Capt. James Smith had just got his guns of the 4th New York Battery, one by one, over the rocks and chasms into an excellent position. After pointing out to Hunt the advancing lines of the enemy, Smith opened fire. In reply, soon many Confederate guns were pounding the exposed ridgeline. Telling Smith he would probably lose his battery, Hunt scrambled back downhill to seek infantry support. Hunt was very doubtful if he would find his horse, for the storm of shell bursting over the ridge was enough to drive any animal wild.

Finally reaching the foot of the steep slope, General Hunt found himself "in a plight at once ludicrous, painful, and dangerous." A herd of horned cattle had been driven into the Plum Run Valley between Devil's Den and Little Round Top, from which they could not escape. A shell exploded, completely tearing one cow to pieces and mangling and wounded several others. The thoroughly frightened animals stampeded, bellowing and rushing in their terror from one side to the other, as they futilely tried to escape the rain of shells that were bursting over and among them. Hunt dodged the careening cattle and finally picked his way through the herd, but he was "badly demoralized" for a moment. Finally locating his horse, he mounted and resumed his duties.

Henry J. Hunt, "Gettysburg Day 2," Century Magazine, December, 1886.

**

As Kershaw's Brigade advanced towards the Rose Farm, a company of the 14th South Carolina Volunteers was sent forward as skirmishers. Crossing a field towards distant Yankees who were protecting a slightly elevated roadway, they discovered a large patch of ripe blackberries. Stooping down, the soldiers kept picking and eating the delicious berries, which were in great abundance on every side. They slowly went forward, their attention fully distracted by the berries. Not until they were within 50 yards of the enemy's advanced line did they realize their position and recall their mission. Whooping the Rebel yell, they surged forward and gained possession of the road, holding it until the rest of the brigade came forward.

Arthur P. Ford, Life in the Confederate Army; Being Personal Experiences of a Private Soldier in the Confederate Army. (New York and Washington: The Neale Publishing Company, 1905).

**

Not all of Kershaw's men accompanied the advance. As the 2nd South Carolina countermarched in obedience to a faulty order, they presented their flank to one of the Union batteries lining the Wheatfield Road. A hail of canister soon greeted the Confederates. The regiment's adjutant suffered a painful wound to one of his feet. William Shumate turned to the stricken officer and offered what aid he could give. The adjutant replied, "Please cut off my boot." Shumate complied, cutting it from top to toe. The adjutant took one last look at the distant battery and immediately fled at a brisk pace to the rear to safety. Shumate and his comrades for years would recall the unusual sight of the officer racing rearward, one naked foot mangled and bleeding, the other still encased in a long cavalry boot. The chagrined adjutant, however, would later coolly deflect all conversation about his Gettysburg footrace.

W. T. Shumate, With Kershaw at Gettysburg: The Experience of a Confederate Private on the 2d of July. (Files of the Gettysburg Discussion Group)

**

The imposing height of Little Round Top was unoccupied by Union troops throughout much of the day, except for some members of the signal corps and staff officers. Seeing a line of Confederates approaching from the west, Brig. Gen. Gouvernor K. Warren sent messengers back to hustle the Fifth Corps to the front. As the 44th New York of Strong Vincent's brigade ran through the fields and woodlots west of Taneytown Road, Sgt. Charles Sprague noticed a cannon ball whiz just above the ears of his major's horse. Soon, the major had dismounted and led his men onward. As the shells burst over the oncoming Federals, a thoroughly frightened fox (the only one Sprague ever saw in the wild) discarded his instinctive fear of men and raced pell-mell through the soldiers, almost under their feet.

Charles E. Sprague, "Military Life as Seen from the Ranks of the Army," Grand Army of the Republic Papers, New York State Archives, Box 25, Folder 18. Used by permission of the University of Albany.

**

Among the Federal troops that rushed to Little Round Top was Col. Strong Vincent's brigade of the Fifth Corps. At the extreme left flank, Col. Joshua L. Chamberlain's 20th Maine held back repeated assaults from Alabama troops commanded by Col. William Oates. One of Oates' men in the 15th Alabama later wrote a personal note to Chamberlain, revealing how close he came to death or injury in the bloody and confused fighting that afternoon:

Dear Sir: I want to tell you of a little passage in the battle of Round Top, Gettysburg, concerning you and me, which I am now glad of. Twice in that fight I had your life in my hands. I got a safe place between two big rocks, and drew a bead fair and square on you. You were standing in the open behind the center of your line, full exposed. I knew your rank by your uniform and your actions, and I thought it a mighty good thing to put you out of the way. I rested my gun on the rock and took steady aim. I started to pull the trigger, but some queer notion stopped me. Then I got ashamed of my weakness and went through the same motions again. I had you perfectly certain. But that same queer something shut right down on me. I couldn't pull the trigger, and I gave up,--that is, your life. I am glad of it now, and hope you are.

Joshua L. Chamberlain, "Through Blood and Fire at Gettysburg. Maine: Her Place in History," Hearst's Magazine, June 1913.

**

Men will often laugh even in the presence of death. As the U.S. Regulars advanced towards Plum Run Valley from Little Round Top, two incidents occurred that caused the solemn soldiers to erupt in laughter despite their prospects for injury or death. A lieutenant in the 14th United States Infantry, much disliked by the men of his regiment, had formerly been a shoemaker by trade. Often the still hours of night (after the playing of Taps) were broken by a peculiarly discordant cry of "Wax! Wax!" emanating from the quarters of the men. Capt. Dudley Chase and the field officers had frequently searched for the offender, but without any success. Now, as the regiment was marching in line down Little Round Top, all hearts strained to their utmost tension, suddenly from their right and rear arose the shrill and ear piercing cry of "Wax! Wax!" A hearty laugh greeted the well-known and familiar sound. It was not until much later that Chase learned the identity of the screamer, who for a moment had broken the mounting tension.

Another lieutenant temporarily attached to Chase's company astonished him as the 14th U.S. was descending the slope, silent and grim. This officer left his customary place in the line and ran along the rear of the company yelling, "Give 'em h---, men! Give 'em h---!" Chase related, "Twice I ordered him to desist, telling him I was in command and to keep quiet. When we made the run across the marsh, this Lieutenant was particularly vociferous, swinging his sword, etc., and in the center of the marsh he fell and was covered with mud. His sword scabbard had gotten between his legs and tripped him. All who saw his misadventure laughed." Soon, the laughter was forgotten as the Confederate bullets began striking home and the realities of war returned.

Capt. Dudley H. Chase, Gettysburg, War Papers, Indiana MOLLUS

**

War was quite personal at times, especially in the armies that comprised fellow Americans separated at times by such short distances. During the afternoon, as Confederate General Ewell's Second Corps artillery dueled with the Union guns on Cemetery Hill, the skies were alive with whizzing and buzzing shells. Lt. James Stewart's Battery B, 4th U.S. Artillery was directly in their range, and received a crossfire of shots from three directions. Nearby, Cooper's Pennsylvania Battery replied, firing towards the distant Benner's Hill. With one of his first shots, he blew up a Rebel caisson. An admiring Stewart ordered his artillerymen to give three cheers for Cooper's battery. The echo had scarcely died away when one of Stewart's own caissons met the same fate, this time to the cheers of the Rebels.

Years later, Stewart reflected on the Southerners' revenge. "It was the cleanest job I ever saw. The three chests were sent skyward and the horses started off on a run toward the town, but one of the swing team got over the traces, throwing him down and causing the rest of the team to halt. The men ran after them and brought them back; every hair was burnt off the tails and manes of the wheel horses. Inquiring for the drivers, the lead and swing drivers reported, but it was some time before I could find out any thing about the wheel driver. One of the men reported that he had seen him go toward the spring. I sent him to hunt him up and tell him to report to me."

A few minutes later, one of Stewart's limbers also exploded, causing a loss of two men and two horses. As Stewart gazed at the shattered limber, an artilleryman came to him with a piece of jacket in his hand and said, "Sir, this is all I call find of Smith, the driver." A month later, Stewart received word that the man was indeed alive, but entirely blind and a patient in a Detroit hospital.

James Stewart, "Battery B Fourth United States Artillery at Gettysburg," Sketches of War History, Ohio MOLLUS Volume 4

**

Brig. Gen. Cadmus Wilcox's men saw hard fighting during the afternoon as they advanced across Emmitsburg Road before finally being repulsed. Wilcox later related an amusing incident from the height of the bitter fighting. Days before the battle, his regiment was resting in camp at Fayetteville, Pennsylvania, in the Cumberland Valley. Fearful that his men would be "gobbled up" and taken prisoner by roving bands of militia and home guards, he issued strict orders against foraging. However, one enterprising noncombatant, a teamster with the 10th Alabama named Pat Martin, disobeyed the order. General Wilcox spotted the "little fellow" slipping through the woods and bushes near headquarters with a string of fine chickens in his hand. Wilcox spoke harshly to him about disobedience of orders and as punishment, removed him from the relative safety of the teamster position and ordered him to rejoin his regiment as a fighting man.

Now on July 2, Wilcox and his brigade were under terrible fire. Several batteries were playing on his command and shells were flying thick and fast. One courier had been killed by Wilcox's side, another seriously wounded. The reins of his horse's bridle had been severed by bullets, and Wilcox found it hard to manage his alarmed mount, which reared and plunged in terror with each new shell burst. Just then, the Alabama general spotted little Pat Martin, who calmly walked towards him in the smoke and noise, leading a group of sixteen Federal prisoners. Halting them near the brigade commander, Martin formed them into line facing the front. Saluting the astonished general with an air of triumph (or perhaps ironic revenge), he said, "Here are your chickens, Sir!"

Edward Alfred Pollard, The Early Life, Campaigns, and Public Services of Robert E. Lee: "With a Record of the Campaigns and Heroic Deeds of his Companions in Arms..." (New York: E. B. Treat & Co., 1871).

**

Pvt. William Alexander of the 15th Alabama had requested temporary service as a mounted courier for Lt. Gen. James Longstreet. At dusk, Maj. John Walton of Vicksburg, an artillery commander under Longstreet, walked up to Alexander, his face powder stained from biting off cartridges. The Mississippian explained to an inquisitive Alexander that his horse had been killed and, now being on foot on the battlefield, he had picked up a musket from a fallen Confederate and joined the fight. Walton then requested Alexander's horse and told him to locate Longstreet's headquarters and wait there for him. Alexander complied with the superior officer's order.

Standing horseless, he gazed around the field looking for a replacement. A nearby Georgia soldier directed his attention to a horse, equipped with saddle and bridle, calmly grazing in no man's land between the lines. Alexander told the infantryman how dangerous it was to try to go get the horse. The Georgian laughed and remarked that it was easy. Accepting the challenge, Alexander crept along on his hands and knees, all the while keeping the horse aligned between himself and the enemy. To his relief, the horse was too tired and hungry to run off when he approached. He quickly mounted the steed, and, lying along his body and neck, sharply dug both spurs into his flank. Several Minié balls whistled by, but Alexander succeeded in returning to the Rebel lines with his new prize. To his chagrin, the animal proved to be a good draft horse, but a poor saddle horse.

Southern Historical Society Papers, Volume 38, pp. 312-18.

**

As darkness descended, the fighting finally waned after multiple desperate Confederate attempts to push through the Union lines. Thousands of wounded and dying men lay in the moonlight; some crying for help or water, others suffering in silence. Lt. Barzilla J. Inman of the 118th Pennsylvania had been struck by a Minié ball during the savage fighting near the Rose Woods. He was lying in a field with a desperately wounded comrade, trapped in no-man's land between the lines and surrounded by dead bodies. An Ohio regiment quietly approached the position, but quickly moved off when they discovered they were so near the Rebel lines. Inman was shocked to discover that stray hogs were rooting among the dead men. Finally, one loudly snorting hog "that in the darkness looked of enormous size" attempted to poke Inman, just as other hogs arrived to investigate the fallen soldier. Inman quickly jammed his sword deep into the belly of the offending pig, which let out a prolonged, sharp cry. The sleepless soldier spent the rest of the night fending off the "monsters" until daylight. He was finally carried off the field on July 4 to recuperate, but was never able to return to active duty.

History of the 118th Pennsylvania Volunteers: Corn Exchange Regiment... (Philadelphia: J. L. Smith, 1905).

**

Company K of the 30th Pennsylvania (commonly known as the First Pennsylvania Reserves) had been recruited in 1861 from Gettysburg and Adams County. For two years, they had witnessed the devastation that war had wrought on Virginia's farmers and townspeople, and now in the summer of 1863, the war had come home to Pennsylvania. As the veteran regiment marched back into Adams County for the first time since it had departed for the training camps, many men passed by their own houses. As they approached Gettysburg, it became evident to others that their homes were now behind enemy lines. Most feared for the safety of their loved ones and friends, which gave the soldiers extra determination to defeat the Rebels and drive them from their home soil.

The regiment formed into battle line near Little Round Top. The German commander of a battery immediately in front of the Reserves' position raved and swore profusely, fearing that his guns would soon be seized by the Confederates. "Dunder und Blixen, don't let dem repels took my batteries," he earnestly appealed in broken English. Brig. Gen. Wiley S. Crawford led the Reserves down the slope and across Plum Run Valley as the exhausted Confederates quickly withdrew under this counterattack. Surging through a stand of trees beyond a stone wall, the 30th paused in the eastern edge of the Wheatfield and reformed. The next morning, the artillery commander came over to the stone wall and appreciatively declared, "The Pennsylvania Reserves saved mine pattery, by Got! I gets you fellers all drunk mit beer."

Henry N. Minnigh's History of Company K 1st (Inft.), Penn'a Reserves "The Boys Who Fought at Home." (Duncansville, PA: "Home Print," 1891).

**

The horrors of war often changed men; sometimes for the good, but often it made them insensitive to life and death. The ground over which the Pennsylvania Reserves had made their attack was strewn with dead Confederates. While passing through a woodlot chasing after the retiring enemy, some of the Bucktails observed "a rascal in a tree from which he killed, during the day, eleven cannoneers. Smoke was seen issuing from the tree whenever he fired, but he managed to conceal his person. He threw his gun down and offered to surrender but the Bucktail couldn't see it in that light. He remarked that those who shot from trees he treated differently and shot him dead on the spot." Mercy was not in the vocabulary of the Pennsylvania marksman that day.

The Columbia (PA) Spy, July 11, 1863.

**

Fighting continued to rage until sunset. In the swirling combat on Little Round Top, Sgt. Charles Sprague had been severely wounded in the left shoulder. He recalled passing by an old stone house in the rear during the 44th New York's hasty advance to the heights. A red flag flying over the building signified that it was a field hospital. Painfully, Sprague walked back to receive aid. As he reached the back door, a "very German person" remarked, "Oh, we can't do noting for you here." Undeterred, Sprague pushed his way into the house,

67

assisted by an able-bodied Confederate who proved more hospitable than the host. The Rebel had stayed behind to assist his wounded commanding general.

Sprague stepped into the middle room, which was the "old folks" bedroom. In front was a parlor, its floor entirely covered with wounded men from both armies. Exhausted from his wound and the long walk, Sprague lay down on the wooden floor, but soon was very uncomfortable, feeling that his unsupported neck was breaking. When a middle-aged woman walked into the room, he asked her to put something under his head, but she didn't understand his request. Luckily, Sprague knew enough German to state, "Etwas unter dem kopf," and in response, she obligingly put some old matting under him.

Bedtime came rather early for the owners. Soon after the firing had ceased for the night, the elderly German host and hostess came into the bedroom and climbed up on their high, fat bed. In the meantime, each wounded soldier lying in the house had adopted some kind of distinctive sound which he repeated at regular intervals. To Sprague, these smothered groans, sighs and breathings - none of them very loud, but intense - recurred often enough to be rather depressing. Soon there were added to the strange concert a particular snore from the old man and another, a different one, by the old woman. And so the wounded passed the night, each repeating his note of endurance, and the "old folks" calmly slept through it all.

The most painful sound was the pleading for "water." Sprague believed that it must have been that Confederate general who repeated it the most. The clock was just as unconcerned as its owners and struck the hours at immensely long intervals. Sprague heard them all, and they were the only sounds he was glad to hear that night. His elderly roommates seemed much refreshed next morning, but he did not see anything more of them, as they went down into the cellar and very sensibly stayed there all the next day during the artillery bombardment. Finally, on the morning of July 4, a younger woman brought warm chicken broth for Sprague and those wounded who still survived.

Charles E. Sprague, "Military Life as Seen from the Ranks of the Army," Grand Army of the Republic Papers, New York State Archives, Box 25, Folder 18. Used by permission of the University of Albany.

**

In the gathering twilight, two of Jubal Early's brigades attacked the Union Eleventh Corps lines on East Cemetery Hill. Fierce hand-to-hand fighting occurred among the Federal batteries near the crest. Portions of Harry Hays's Louisiana Tigers as well as Ike Avery's North Carolina brigade managed to reach the guns after driving off several Union regiments. As the 153rd Pennsylvania of Von Gilsa's brigade rallied, they witnessed a wild melee between the oncoming Rebels and the gun crews of Battery I, 1st New York Light Artillery (Weidrich's Battery). Clubs, knives, guns, fists – the soldiers and cannoneers used whatever weapons they had at their disposal. One daring Southerner reached a field piece and draped himself over the muzzle, while crying out to the remaining gunners "I take command of this gun!" A sturdy German artillerist, in the act of firing the gun, curtly replied, "Du sollst die haben" ("You can have this!") and yanked the lanyard. A second later, the soul of the reckless Confederate had taken flight. Within minutes, the remaining Rebels began to withdraw, many frustrated that no fresh supporting troops were to be seen. Within two weeks, the 153rd Pennsylvania was no more, as its term of enlistment expired on July 13. They were soon met with a hero's welcome in Harrisburg.

William R. Kiefer, History of the One Hundred and Fifty-third Regiment Regiment Pennsylvania Volunteers Which was Recruited in Northampton County, Pa. 1862-1863. The Chemical Publishing Co. 1909.

**

Confederate partisan cavalry officer Harry Gilmor, bored with scouting duties and eager as always for a fight, left his regiment and volunteered to join the Louisiana Tigers' assault on the heights. He was an eyewitness to the swirling and confused twilight melee on East Cemetery Hill, which had once been a peaceful picnic area for the locals. "I saw one of our color-bearers jump on a gun and display his flag. He was instantly killed. But the flag was seized by an Irishman, who, with a wild shout, sprang upon the gun, and he too was shot down. Then a little bit of a fellow, a captain, seized the staff and mounted the same gun; but, as he raised the flag, a ball broke the arm which held it. He dropped his sword and caught the staff with his right hand before it fell, waved it over his head with a cheer, indifferent to the pain of his shattered limb and the whizzing balls around him. His third cheer was just heard, when he tottered and fell, pierced through the lungs."

Harry Gilmor, Four Years in the Saddle. (New York: Harper & Brothers, 1866).

**

Devastation and destruction marked the paths of the opposing armies, and the piteous cries of the wounded filled the air. Many Gettysburg residents freely opened their homes and offered comfort to the injured and ill. Elizabeth Thorn and her family lived in the Evergreen Cemetery Gatehouse. Her husband Peter was serving in the Union army in the Washington defenses, and she and her parents kept up the cemetery grounds. On July 1, they had been ordered off the property by Federal Maj. Gen. Oliver O. Howard, who feared for their safety and was now using their home as his headquarters. The pregnant Mrs. Thorn, her three small children (Fred age 7, George age 5, and John age 2) and her elderly parents walked south of town to the Musser farm, where they sought shelter and food.

Shortly after midnight on July 2, she and her father decided to walk home to the gatehouse. As they left the Musser house, they passed through a room where wounded Union soldiers were sleeping, lying in two rows, with a solitary candle to light the whole room. About the middle of one row, a man raised himself on his elbow and motioned for Elizabeth to come to him. When her father signaled that it was all right, she went to the stricken man. He took a picture out of his pocket and showed it to Mrs. Thorn. It portrayed three little boys and he said they were his. They were just little boys like hers, and would she please allow her sons to sleep near him?

A sympathetic Elizabeth left her sons lying next to the homesick soldier and walked up Baltimore Pike to the gatehouse, which she found in considerable disarray inside. Wounded soldiers filled the yard and the interior. She and her father gathered what few possessions they could carry, returned to the Musser house and picked up the children before heading further out of town. Weeks later, Elizabeth and her father would dig nearly 100 graves in the July heat to bury soldiers that had died on the cemetery property. Her baby was delivered safely three months later, but her health was broken from the arduous task of burying the dead.

Elizabeth Thorn account, Gettysburg National Military Park

**

Many of the soldiers could not venture out to creeks and streams to fetch water due to enemy skirmishers. After dark, Color Sgt. Daniel Crotty and his comrades in the 3rd Michigan slipped off to find the nearest source to brew some coffee. With the hard rains of recent days, they found that a cow's tracks in a nearby field still had standing water. Using a spoon to dip it up, they labored for an hour until they had sufficient liquid for a pot of coffee, which they drank "with a hearty relish" as it was the first they had enjoyed since leaving Emmitsburg. What water was around their lines was "reserved for the wounded, and of course the officers."

D. G. Crotty, Four Years of Campaigning in the Army of the Potomac, (Grand Rapids, MI: Dygert Bros. & Co., 1874).

**

Throughout the long, hot night, jittery sentries and pickets occasionally fired at shadows, fearing an enemy attack. In one case, an entire regiment fired a volley. According to Col. Rufus Dawes of the 6th Wisconsin of the Iron Brigade, "It is a troubled and dreamy sleep at best that comes to the soldier on a battle field. About one o'clock at night we had a great alarm. A man in the Seventh Indiana Regiment, next on our right, cried so loudly in his sleep that he aroused all the troops in the vicinity. Springing up, half bewildered, I ordered my regiment to 'fall in,' and a heavy fire of musketry broke out from along the whole line of men." Luckily, no one was harmed by this useless waste of government-issued ammunition. The soldiers went back to sleep, no doubt concerned what the morrow might bring.

Rufus R. Dawes, "With the Sixth Wisconsin at Gettysburg," Sketches of War History, Ohio MOLLUS, Volume 3

Chapter 4

The Battle of Gettysburg
Friday, July 3, 1863

At dawn, fighting erupted along Culp's Hill, where repeated Confederate attempts to seize the Union breastworks had essentially failed the previous night. Lt. Randolph McKim, a staff officer in Steuart's Brigade, narrowly escaped serious injury. A Minié ball grazed his shoulder as he was bringing ammunition up the slope to waiting comrades. Soon, another passed through his haversack and ripped the back cover off of a New Testament he had in a pocket. A spent shell fragment ricocheted off a tree and struck McKim in the back, leaving a large welt. As the Confederates formed into line for one final assault, another bullet struck him on the wrist. The impact violently threw his entire arm around and caused sharp pain. "Your arm is broken, is it not, Lieutenant?" said Col. E.T.H. Warren of the 10th Virginia. "I don't know yet," replied McKim as he took off his gauntlet. Inwardly McKim was thinking, "I hope it is. I'd be glad to compromise with the loss of an arm to get out of this hopeless charge." To his dismay, he found that he had no excuse for not going forward on the charge. No bones were broken and no blood had been spilled. He did have a large "red and angry looking" lump over the wrist bones. The ball had struck a sturdy brass button on the glove and had glanced aside, avoiding more serious damage. Ironically, he was wearing gauntlets with brass buttons because of a trade orchestrated by his cousin, who had preferred McKim's plain gloves. Despite his reluctance, he made the charge, which was readily repulsed. McKim survived the battle without further injury. Four close calls were enough for the young officer.

Randolph H. McKim, A Soldier's Recollections: Leaves from the Diary of a Young Confederate. (New York: Longmans, Green, and Co., 1910).

**

As with most armies of the day and the lack of reliable information, wild rumors soon began circulating among the troops and officials of both sides. One had veteran Confederate General James Longstreet as being killed or captured. New Jersey Gov. Joel Parker was leading a campaign to have former Union army commander George McClellan reinstated, and some in the Federal ranks kept this hope alive with stories that the general had been spotted at headquarters. Perhaps the most ill-advised rumor was relayed by Maj. Gen.

Darius Couch, a veteran who had capably led the Second Army Corps until he had a falling out with army commander Joseph Hooker and resigned in May. Seizing upon doubtful information without first obtaining verification, he sent a laughable telegram to the Secretary of War in Washington.

HARRISBURG, PA., July 3, 1863 – 9:30 a. m. (Received 10:20 a.m.)

Honorable E. M. STANTON:

Jefferson Davis was undoubtedly at Greencastle yesterday.

D. N. COUCH,
Major-General.

At the time, President Davis was safely ensconced in his office in downtown Richmond, nearly 200 miles from the Pennsylvania town. Couch's credibility suffered a blow.

The War of the Rebellion: A Compilation of the Official Records of the Union and Confederate Armies, 70 volumes in 4 series. Washington, D.C.: United States Government Printing Office, 1880-1901. Volume 39, The Gettysburg Campaign.

** **

Following the repulse of the Confederate attacks around Little Round Top the previous day and the loss of their brigadier general, the 155th Pennsylvania of Weed's Brigade was lounging during the morning of July 3. Many soldiers played euchre or similar card games. Some smoked and conversed or read newspapers, while others wrote letters or penned their thoughts in journals and diaries. One artistic soldier busily drew portraits of Union generals George Meade and G. K. Warren in his sketchbook. However, Maj. Alfred L. Pearson's relaxation was short-lived. A delegation of citizen farmers living adjacent to Little Round Top had entered the camp to present their grievances.

Apparently uncaring about the carnage and human suffering that now surrounded the region, they bitterly complained that the army had confiscated the straw and hay in their barns for use in the hastily organized field hospitals to comfort the wounded. They demanded immediate compensation for their loss. A shocked and angered Pearson delivered a stinging rebuke, denouncing in strong language their lack of patriotism and inhumanity. He ordered the committee of farmers to leave Little Round Top, with the warning that if they did not do so, he would personally order the 155th to march down the slope and torch their barns, while subjecting the farmers to a formal court-martial for disloyalty.

Pearson's threats apparently did not deter the farmers for very long. On Saturday morning, the same men made the rounds of the field hospitals, demanding that the surgeons produce cash in compensation for the procured straw and hay. Pearson later bitterly lamented "the dense ignorance of these peasants," whose lack of concern for the sufferings of the wounded exhibited a "total want of public spirit." They never received any recompense from the army or the government for their loss.

Under the Maltese cross, Antietam to Appomattox: The Loyal Uprising in Western Pennsylvania, 1861-1865; Campaigns of the 155th Pennsylvania Regiment, narrated by the rank and file. (Pittsburgh: The 155th Regimental Association, 1910).

**

Other soldiers took the lull in the action as an opportunity to take care of some necessary personal health issues. The 16th Michigan Volunteer Infantry had remained on Little Round Top until 10 o'clock in the morning, when they were relieved. Marching half a mile to the right in the direction of Cemetery Hill, in thirty minutes they had constructed a good solid breastwork. With everything quiet in this new position, Lt. Ziba Graham received permission to go back to the division hospital to get an ugly tooth extracted, one that had kept him dancing in pain all the night before. The regimental surgeon, Doctor Everett, who had been hard at work all night at the amputation table, made but short work and little ado about one tooth. He quickly laid Graham on the ground, straddled him, and with a formidable pair of nippers pulled and yanked his head around until the offending tooth came free. Daunted by this quick but painful work, Graham made up his mind never to go to a surgeon for a tooth pulling matinee the day after a fight.

Ziba B. Graham, "On to Gettysburg: Ten Days from My Diary," War Papers, Michigan MOLLUS, Volume 1
**

Two men of the 6th Pennsylvania Reserves found a horse tied in the woods near the Wheatfield. They brought the abandoned animal back into their lines. A youngster named Dan Cole, to relieve the monotony of picket-firing, mounted the animal and rode down in front of the brigade lines, between the opposing forces lampooning Col. Buck McCandless, the brigade commander. He appealed in the most pathetic tones to the boys to remember their "daddies" and "mammies" and "best gal," and "never to desert the old flag as long as there was a ration left." He created much amusement until the horse bounced him off and scampered over to the Rebels, when the cheers and shouts of both lines caused the men to forget for the moment they were enemies.

Pennsylvania at Gettysburg: Ceremonies at the dedication of the monuments erected by the commonwealth of Pennsylvania... (Pennsylvania Battlefield Commission, 1913).

**

The battlefield was eerily quiet in the noon hour as soldiers on both sides pondered their fate, for it was clear that the fighting was not over. In the center, Robert E. Lee had massed artillery to try to drive off the Union guns from Cemetery Ridge. About 1:00 p.m., two Confederate lone guns fired, signaling to the other batteries to commence firing. One of the shells from the signal guns whistled far over the Union lines and burst in William Patterson's barn near the Taneytown Road. The explosion mangled the arm of a 14-year-old free black boy, a servant of an officer in a New York infantry regiment. The surgeon of the nearby Clark's Battery was summoned to amputate the teenager's limb. He was loaded into an ambulance and accompanied the battery to a safer environ.

Michael Hanifen, History of Battery B, First New Jersey Artillery. (Ottawa, Illinois: Republican-Times, 1905).

**

The Confederate army was accompanied by some foreign officers, including a Captain Schreiber of the Austrian army and Lt. Col. Sir Arthur Fremantle of the famed British Coldstream Guards. After a brief stopover in Cuba, Fremantle had arrived in Texas on April 1. He had spent considerable time exploring Confederate fortresses and armies during a wandering sojourn through several Southern states. In mid-June, he had caught up with Lee's army on its northward trek. Determined to watch Longstreet's attack on July 3, Fremantle and Schreiber headed for downtown Gettysburg to a building with a cupola, which promised a splendid vantage point to watch Longstreet's men step off. However, soon after passing through the tollgate on the Chambersburg Pike, they found that they were riding into a heavy crossfire, and shells, both from Federal and Confederate guns, frequently passed over their heads.

Continuing to ride through the streets, they became alarmed when two shells burst close to them, spraying shrapnel through the air. A fragment smashed into the Confederate officer who was escorting the pair of European observers. They quickly wheeled their horses and headed back to the Rebel lines, where only the Union shells would be a bother. A small 12-year-old boy was riding with them. In Fremantle's words, "This urchin took a diabolical interest in the bursting of the shells, and screamed with delight when he saw them take effect. I never saw this boy again, or found out who he was."

Sir Arthur James Lyon Fremantle, Three Months in the Southern States: April, June, 1863. (Mobile: S. H. Goetzel, 1864)

**

A staff member of Maj. Gen. John Sedgwick of the Sixth Corps, Thomas Hyde, had posted himself on some rocks along the crest of Cemetery Ridge observing the distant Confederate line. Soon, Generals Meade and Warren came up on the rocks to take a look, and Hyde dodged back to tell Sedgwick that it looked like a cannonade would soon erupt. About noon, the officers were sitting in a field strewn with boulders and some small trees, enjoying a simple lunch of hardtack and coffee, when two guns were fired from the enemy's side. Hyde quickly concluded he did not want any more lunch and ducked behind a boulder large enough to cover himself and his horse. The open ground behind the Union line was being torn up in every direction by the shells. Occasionally a caisson exploded, riderless horses were dashing about, and a throng of wounded streamed to the rear.

When the cannonade was at its height and everyone of judgment was utilizing what cover he could find, Hyde was astonished to see a lone figure leisurely walking over the plain behind his position. The ground which was being beaten into dust in every direction by the enemy's shells, yet on came the distant figure. As he neared, Hyde could make him out to be a man with a long beard and spectacles, wearing a brown linen duster. When he got a little nearer, he saw that the seemingly foolhardy figure was the sutler's clerk, who was staggering in his gait. As the clerk neared Hyde, a shell shrieked by, making more than the usual fiendish noise. He looked down at Hyde, put his hand up to his ear, and said, "Listen to the mocking-bird." With the providential good fortune of drunken men, he had crossed for some distance in safety over ground where it seemed impossible for any living thing to remain a minute.

Thomas W. Hyde, "Recollections of the Battle of Gettysburg," War Papers, Maine MOLLUS, Volume 1, September 1892.

**

It was during this fierce cannonade that one Napoleon gun of Battery B, 1st Rhode Island Light Artillery was struck by a Confederate shell that exploded and killed two artillerymen who were loading the brass piece. William Jones, the Number 1 crewman, had stepped to his assigned place between the muzzle of the piece and the right wheel, and had swabbed the gun and was waiting for the charge to be inserted. Alfred Gardner, the No. 2, was on the left side facing to the rear, taking the ammunition from No. 5 over the wheel. He turned slightly to the left, and was inserting the charge into the piece when an enemy shell struck the left side of the muzzle and exploded. Jones died instantly when a shell fragment struck the left side of his head. He fell with his battered head toward the enemy, and the sponge staff was thrown forward beyond him two or three yards. Gardner was struck in the left shoulder, almost tearing his arm from his body. He fell at his post, but with the other arm he drew from his pocket a Testament and a little book which he carried with him to press flowers, and handing them to his sergeant said, "Give these to my wife, and tell her that I died happy - glory, glory, hallelujah!" He lived a few minutes and died shouting, "Glory to God! I am happy! Hallelujah!"

The sergeant of the piece, Albert Straight, and the remaining cannoneers tried to load the damaged piece and placed a charge in the muzzle of the gun. They found it impossible to ram it home. Again and again they tried to drive home the charge which proved so obstinate, but their efforts were futile. The depression on the muzzle was so great that the charge could not be forced in and the attempt was abandoned. As the piece cooled off, the shot became firmly fixed in the bore of the gun. The gun, with the cannonball still firmly lodged in the bore, was sent to the rear, and then later forwarded to the arsenal at Washington, DC, where it was placed on exhibition. For decades since, it has been on display in Rhode Island.

John H. Rhodes, "The Gettysburg Gun," Personal Narratives of the Rebellion, Rhode Island MOLLUS, 4th Series, No.19

**

The day before, Second Corps infantryman Warren Goss had recorded the peaceful idyllic scenery in this pastoral valley. Now, the panorama had dramatically changed. Capt. Samuel Fiske reported a much different vista, one scarred by the howling mechanisms of warfare. "It was touching to see the little birds, all out of their wits with fright, flying wildly about amidst the tornado of terrible missiles and uttering strange notes of distress. It was touching to see the innocent cows and calves, feeding in the fields, torn in pieces by the shells."

Samuel Fiske, Mr. Dunn Browne's Experiences in the Army. (Boston: Nichols and Noyes, 1866).

**

With the eventual cessation of the prolonged mutual cannonade, three divisions of Confederate infantry stepped off from the Seminary Ridge area and headed across nearly a mile of ground towards the Union lines on Cemetery Ridge and Cemetery Hill. Lt. Col. Rawley W. Martin was an officer in Armistead's Brigade within George Pickett's division. He later wrote, "The esprit du corps could not have been better; the men were in good physical condition, self reliant and determined. They felt the gravity of the situation, for they knew well the metal of the foe in their front; they were serious and resolute, but not disheartened. None of the usual jokes, common on the eve of battle, were indulged in, for every man felt his individual responsibility, and realized that he had the most stupendous work of his life before him; officers and men knew at what cost and at what risk the advance was to be made, but they had deliberately made up their minds to attempt it. I believe the general sentiment of the division was that they would succeed in driving the Federal line from what was their objective point; they knew that many, very many, would go down under the storm of shot and shell which would greet them when their gray ranks were spread out to view, but it never occurred to them that disaster would come after they once placed their tattered banners upon the crest of Seminary Ridge."

Martin witnessed several instances of individual coolness and bravery exhibited in the charge. Under intense fire, his regiment, the 53rd Virginia, maintained almost parade ground dress order early in the advance. Soon, the pounding Federal artillery began to tear holes in the Confederate lines. Capt. Henry Edmunds and the entirety of Company F were thrown flat to the earth by the explosion of a shell hurtled from Little Round Top. Every man who was not killed or desperately wounded sprang to his feet, collected himself and moved forward to close the gap made in the regimental front. Later as the regiment drew within musket range of the Federals, a soldier from the same regiment was shot in the shin. He stopped in the midst of the terrific fire, rolled up his pants leg, calmly examined his wound, and then went forward with his comrades up to the stone wall.

Richmond Times-Dispatch, April 10, 1904.

**

As the Confederates advanced, they flushed before them a bevy of Union skirmishers in the fields just west of the Emmitsburg Road, including those of the 19th Maine. These skirmishers had lain in position from sunrise to 3:00 p.m. on their faces in the burning sun, and according to Capt. Silas Adams, "We were pretty well cooked through. When the enemy came near us we arose and started for the rear, and I can speak only from my own experience in describing my attempt to walk. I found I had no use of my legs, having lain so long that they had become numb or paralyzed, but in a few moments they got into working order so I could trudge slowly to the rear. The men held their relative positions at fifteen paces while going there." With the Rebels closing in, Adams' men hurled a few Minié balls at their pursuers, with most of the Maine men getting off at least a couple of shots, not drawing a response from the lengthy Confederate line. In the meantime, Federal officers along the main line, not understanding that the skirmishers suffered from cramps and numbness, called them to come in quickly so they could fire. Some portions of the Union line even fired upon Adams and his comrades, thinking them actually to be Rebel skirmishers as they kept pace with the gray and butternut-clad line. Finally, the men began to painfully run into their lines, luckily without any casualties from friendly fire.

Capt. Silas Adams, "The Nineteenth Maine at Gettysburg," War Papers, Maine MOLLUS, Volume 4

**

At the stone wall and along much of the Federal line, fighting was at close quarters. Death and injury became very personal, as soldiers were often locked in hand-to-hand combat. Col. Birkett D. Fry commanded what was left of Archer's Brigade during the Confederate advance. He later related, "As evidence of how close was the fighting at that part of the line, I saw a Federal soldier with an ugly wound in his shoulder, which he told me he received from the spear on the end of one of my regimental colors; and I remembered having that morning observed and laughingly commented on the fact that the color-bearer of the Thirteenth Alabama had attached to his staff a formidable-looking lance head." Spear points, bayonets, swords, pistols, knives, rocks, fists, and muskets – all were employed in a frantic effort to dislodge the enemy.

B. D. Fry, Montgomery, Alabama, December 14th, 1878. (Southern Historical Society Papers, Volume 7, pp. 91-93).

**

In battle, death and injury can come in many strange ways. Most of the officers in the three divisions that made up the fabled charge went in on foot. However, a handful, including Col. Lewis B. Williams of the 1st Virginia in Kemper's Brigade, chose to ride. Mounted on a little bay mare, Williams flourished his steel sword and encouraged his men onward. Near the brick Codori farmhouse, he was suddenly knocked out of the saddle by a Minié ball in the shoulder. In a bizarre twist, the wounded officer was killed as he fell, impaled on his sword. His riderless horse kept on with the men in the charge, eventually returning to the Rebel lines limping and sadly crippled according to eyewitness Col. Joseph Mayo of the 3rd Virginia. Mayo saw this same mare again at Williamsport in care of Williams' slave Harry, who asked him what he thought his old master would say when the horse was all that remained from "Marse Lewis's" belongings to take home.

Richmond Times-Dispatch, May 6, 1906.

**

In small knots and singly, the defeated Confederates withdrew across the fields back to Seminary Ridge. Capt. Robert Bright of Pickett's staff was with Gen. James Longstreet when the visiting English officer, Sir Arthur Fremantle, rode up at half-speed, reining his horse immediately in front of the general. Fremantle exclaimed, "General Longstreet, General Lee sent me here, and said you would place me in a position to see this magnificent charge. I would not have missed it for the world." General Longstreet wearily answered, "I would, Colonel Fremantle, the charge is over. Captain Bright, ride to General Pickett, and tell him what you have heard me say to Colonel Fremantle." The so-called High Tide of the Confederacy had ebbed.

Richmond Times-Dispatch, February 7, 1904.

**

General Lee, anguished over the setback, nevertheless remained a careful observer of his men as they withdrew to the cover of Seminary Ridge. Seeing a nearby officer beat a horse that had been badly frightened by a shell burst, Lee remarked, "Don't whip him, Captain – don't whip him; I've got such another foolish horse myself, and whipping does no good." Nearby, a terrified soldier lay facedown in a ditch. Colonel Fremantle remarked to Lee that he did not think the man was dead. Lee's attention was drawn to the man, who suddenly began groaning dismally, as if in his death throes. When Lee's appeals to the man's patriotism went unanswered, he ordered some nearby artillerymen to grab the prostrated soldier and set him on his feet.

Sir Arthur James Lyon Fremantle, Three Months in the Southern States: April, June, 1863. (Mobile: S. H. Goetzel, 1864)

**

Two brigades had been ordered to advance on Pickett's right flank – the Alabamans of Cadmus Wilcox and a small brigade of Floridians under Col. David Lang. Both supporting attacks were rather handily repulsed, mostly with concentrated artillery fire. A number of soldiers fell dead or injured. Among the latter was Pvt. Lewis Powell of Company I, 2nd Florida Infantry. He was sent to a Federal prisoner-of-war camp and was exchanged later in the war, when he joined Mosby's Rangers (the 53rd Virginia Cavalry), a famed group of partisans and guerilla fighters. Tired of army life, he later moved to Baltimore, Maryland, where he assumed the alias "Lewis Paine."

He was a key member of John Wilkes Booth's inner circle of conspirators in the Lincoln assassination. On the night of April 14, 1865, Powell/Paine viciously attacked U.S. Secretary of State William Seward. He bullied his way into Seward's home and stabbed the cabinet member repeatedly as he lay sick in his bed. Seward managed to survive the attack, although it left him terribly scarred. Powell's escape attempt was thwarted and he was found guilty and hanged on July 7, 1865. After his execution, no relatives showed up to claim his body. His skull wound up forgotten and uncatalogued in the Smithsonian Institution's vast collection before being rediscovered in 1992. Two years later, Powell's skull was released to a relative and buried in Florida next to his mother's grave.

Files of the Gettysburg National Military Park

**

By the late afternoon, both armies were exhausted and casualties were horrendous. In several cases, regiments had become separated from their supply wagons, many of which were still behind in Westminster, Maryland. Soldiers were hot, tired, worn out from stress and the heat, and often quite hungry. The 121st Pennsylvania had fought long and hard on July 1 before withdrawing through Gettysburg, leaving nearly 180 of their comrades behind as casualties. They had taken a reserve position near the Taneytown Road, where they endured the artillery overshooting before Pickett's Charge. Food supplies were gone and the soldiers were famished, most not having eaten since leaving Emmitsburg on June 30. Luckily, a green-clad regiment of Berdan's Sharpshooters was marching along the road not far from the 121st's position. Halting to rest, the marksmen soon discovered that the 121st had no food. They generously opened their haversacks and shared their contents, an act of kindness remembered for years by the Pennsylvanians.

History of the 121st Pennsylvania Volunteers: An Account from the Ranks. (Villanova, PA: W.W. Strong, 1905).

Chapter 5

The Aftermath

Throughout the day of July 4, scattered skirmishing and firefights occurred, as well as occasional Federal forays to probe the strength of parts of the Confederate lines. Sniping marked several parts of the battlefield. Pvt. William Warren and his comrades in Company C of the 17th Connecticut were on skirmish duty near East Cemetery Hill. Towards Gettysburg, they could see an old well near a brick house, which they presumed was being used by the Rebel officers that commanded their picket line. A number of times during Independence Day, thirsty Rebel soldiers would cautiously approach the well and crank the old fashioned windlass to raise the bucket. The Federal soldiers would allow them to get the bucket most of the way up before unleashing a torrent of Minié balls, which would send the Southerners scattering for safety behind the house. The process would be repeated at intervals, a sport of great amusement to the Nutmegs, but "probably it was not much fun for the thirsty Johnnies."

William H. Warren, Seventeenth Connecticut: The Record of a Yankee Regiment in the War for the Union. (Published in 1886 by the Danbury Times, Bridgeport Public Library's Historical Collections).

**

Soon it became clear that neither army commander truly wished to resume the hostilities. Individual acts of bravery and daring were still common, however, on this Saturday. During the morning, Pvt. Henry "Harry" Shaler of Indianapolis slipped a nondescript poncho over his blue uniform coat so that the Confederates would not readily identify him as a Federal soldier. Pretending to be one of their own, he approached a group of 18 Rebel infantrymen and ordered them to lay down their arms and help carry wounded from the still teeming fields. Most did without resistance. After separating them from their weapons, Shaler rode over to the lieutenant in charge and ordered him to surrender his sword. Being refused, Harry flashed a hidden "pepper-box" pistol, which convinced the Confederate to surrender. Shaler took his captives back to the Union camp; then using the same ruse, later corralled a captain and five more enlisted men.

Frank Moore, Anecdotes, Poetry, and Incidents of the War: North and South. 1860-1865. (New York: Publication office, Bible house, J. Porteus, agent, 1867).

**

On Cemetery Hill, the town's Evergreen Cemetery was a shambles, the once peaceful graveyard now torn and mangled with the marks of war. Graves and grass had been trampled by horses' hooves. Headstones and memorial markers had been overturned (at times by Union soldiers to prevent their destruction, and at times by shell bursts which had shattered a few stones, as well as a family shaft). The well-manicured shrubbery had vanished and was now a withered mass of tangled brushwood. Iron fences that surrounded family plots were missing or mangled. The badly decomposing carcass of a horse sprawled across one resident's grave. Over another were the torn and soiled garments of a fallen soldier, their remnants drenched with dried blood. Perhaps most poignantly, fragments of a musket shattered by an exploding shell now adorned the small head-stone that bore the sad words, "To the memory of our beloved child, Mary."

Thomas W. Knox, Camp-fire and Cotton-field: Southern Adventure in Time of War. Life with the Union Armies… (New York: Blelock and Company, 1865).

**

As the surviving Federal soldiers realized that the Confederates were retreating, jubilation spread through the ranks. Many regiments formally cheered, and shouts of "Huzzah! Huzzah! Huzzah!" soon echoed across the still bloody fields. Other regiments broke out supplies of whiskey and other delicacies. In some cases, local produce, chickens, hams, and other foodstuffs soon emerged around campfires as soldiers began foraging. For the men of the 96th Pennsylvania, the reward was quite different. Capt. Samuel R. Russel wrote to his mother on July 4, "The men are in splendid spirits. The smell of the dead is awful. We have not had time to bury them. We will wind up the rebel army before they reach the Potomac. We have all got sixty-five crackers to celebrate the day with. I must close." They had just fought and won the largest battle in American history, and as a reward, each man had received pieces of hardtack to munch.

Pottsville Miners' Journal, July 12, 1863.

**

Some soldiers took the time to hunt for souvenirs among the discarded material littering the field and hospitals. In one downtown warehouse turned into a temporary hospital, one Federal nurse rifled through the knapsack of a dead Rebel and found a well-traveled Bible. On the cover was the inscription, "Miss Almira Alice Wilson, Presque Island, August 18, '52" (or '62 as he could not discern the exact year). Opening the clasp, to his amusement, he noted a variety of names inscribed on it in addition to Miss Wilson's. On the flyleaf was written "Moses C. Ames" (or Amors). On the opposite page was "Wm. M. Nichols, company F, 21st Regiment, Georgia V. I., May 27, 1863." On the last leaf and back cover was inscribed "William Martin Nichols' Book; picked up on the battle-field near Chancellorsville, May 31, 1863." The new owner then took out a pen and added his own commentary, "Taken from the knapsack of a dead rebel at Warehouse Hospital, Gettysburg, July 1863." He surmised that the Bible had been given as a keepsake by the Maine woman to a friend, who had perished at Chancellorsville in a Union regiment. Private Nichols had picked it up, then he or yet another Rebel had carried it to Gettysburg. The nurse would later seek to return the wandering testament to Miss Wilson.

Frank Moore, Anecdotes, Poetry, and Incidents of the War: North and South. 1860-1865. (New York: Publication office, Bible house, J. Porteus, agent, 1867).

**

In places where it was safe to do so, Union soldiers began venturing out in the fields and woods where the Rebel dead and wounded still lay thick. In many cases, the Yankees were looking for plunder, taking knives, wallets, coins, food, buttons and the like from their enemies. Sometimes, the relics were more personal. One soldier picked up and kept a small piece of paper that contained two locks of hair. The sheet was addressed in flowing feminine handwriting to a "Mr. Wellerford," from Louisiana, apparently by his wife. Below one lock was written "Fanny Wellerford;" below the other tuft was "Richard Wellerford." At the bottom of the page was the poignant phrase, "Our Darlings!" The owner had apparently carried this memento of home with him to Pennsylvania, where it may have fluttered out of his dying grasp. He was never identified, and probably was buried in one of the trenches along Culp's Hill or along Cemetery Hill, where the Louisianans suffered their most casualties. No one by that name appears, however, on the muster rolls of Gettysburg casualties.

Richard Miller, The Pictorial Book of Anecdotes and Incidents of the War of the Rebellion, Civil, Military, Naval and Domestic... (Hartford, CT: Hartford Publishing Company, 1867).

**

Curiosity and souvenir hunting were of particular interest to many citizens and soldiers. However, food was still paramount in the minds of many men who had not eaten during the height of the battle. Early Saturday morning, a squad of men of the First Corps commissary department drove a young heifer to the camp of the 80th New York and butchered it on the grounds. They distributed several boxes of hardtack and some coffee, sugar, and salt. By the time the beef was cut up, the men had their fires going and coffee ready and the meat was speedily distributed and cooked. Soon, there was nothing left of the heifer (the intestines being buried) but the hide. To Capt. John Cook, "It was an amusing sight to see the farm-boys of the neighborhood getting these hides. The one near us was seized by a solid-looking chap about twelve years old, who took the tail over his shoulder and whose strength was taxed to the utmost as he hauled it away. In the course of the morning I saw several others gathered by boys in the same way. They manifested little curiosity as to the soldiers or interest in the battle, and either did not think of what they could pick up on the field or were afraid to try it. But there were beef-hides. They knew these were valuable, and, as nobody objected, they secured them and hauled them away by the tails as their share of the spoil." The boys could sell these hides to the local tanneries for decent money.

John D. S. Cook, "Personal Remembrances of Gettysburg," War Talks in Kansas, Kansas MOLLUS, Volume 1.

**

Still encamped at Gettysburg on July 4, some Federal soldiers were disgusted by the attitude of certain local farmers, who sought to use the presence of the army for personal financial gain. One correspondent in the Pennsylvania Reserves wrote, "Here is a farmer who has twelve stray cows, all of which he has milked daily, in addition to his own, whose farm and crops have been protected from the hands of the despoiler, by the blood of the slain, and whose barn is filled with two hundred bleeding dying patriots. Does he give them milk when they ask for and plead for it? Yes, at five cents a pint! Does he give them one loaf of bread when they have saved for him ten thousand? Yes. At forty cents a loaf. Here is another who has been driven from his home by the invading hosts, who bought tobacco at eight cents a plug, and sells it to the wounded at fifteen. Bought letter paper at a cent per sheet, and taking advantage of their misfortune, sells it to the disabled at five - all this because they have unfortunately fell defending his home. They seem to be proud of the opportunity, and laugh at their cunning in counting their gains - it is not cunning, it is something less then duplicity."

Lancaster (PA) Daily Express, July 13, 1863.

**

For thousands of seriously wounded soldiers, food was the farthest thing from their mind as they struggled to survive. Capt. Jack Adams of the 19th Massachusetts infantry had been badly wounded on July 2. He had eventually been moved to the rear along Taneytown Road, where a surgeon pronounced that he would not survive 24 hours. Enduring the Confederate artillery bombardment on July 3, he had convinced an officer to order some noncombatants to move him farther to the rear to safety. To the amazement of the doctors, he did not die, and slowly began regaining his strength even though he was lying on the open ground. Still, he was left behind when the Second Corps hospitals were moved again.

Fearing that he would not get the medical attention that he needed, Adams and two colleagues pooled their cash and found that they had $10 to spend. They managed to find a local farmer, who agreed to convey them to a church in nearby Littlestown, Pennsylvania, where private doctors and nurses were ministering to the wounded. The price for the jaunt was steep, as it cost them all their funds and Adams felt that he could have bought the old spring-wagon and the nag for that exorbitant amount. The trio was soon convalescing on temporary "beds," boards laid across pews in a church. Adams recovered and returned home. Later in the war, he spent nine months in Confederate prisoner of war camps, including an escape and recapture.

Capt. John G. B. Adams, Reminiscences of the Nineteenth Massachusetts Regiment. (Boston: Wright, Potter Printing Company, 1899).

**

A massive thunderstorm on the evening of July 4 drenched the armies, creating untold misery and torture for the thousands of wounded that still dotted the fields and woods surrounding Gettysburg. Creeks and streams, already swollen from days of rain before the Battle of Gettysburg, swiftly overflowed their banks, and flash floods claimed the lives of scores of unfortunate wounded men. The hospital of Clark's Battery was in a field near Rock Creek east of Taneytown Road. The attendants and orderlies frantically worked to move the injured soldiers to higher ground. However, the water rose so quickly that not all could be moved. Artilleryman Dick Price held himself up above the torrent with his elbows draped over the branch of a dogwood tree. The lower extremities of both arms had been amputated, so Price's agony must have been excruciating. Still, he held his composure. Noting a wounded comrade, Billy Riley, who was climbing another nearby tree, Price called out, "Billy, they talk about Napoleon climbing the Alps, why isn't there a marker to Dick Price climbing the dogwood?" However, Price would soon die from complications resulting from his wounds. He is buried in the National Cemetery.

Michael Hanifen, History of Battery B, First New Jersey Artillery. (Ottawa, Illinois: Republican-Times, 1905).

**

One wounded member of Pickett's Division, Lt. James F. Crocker, was quite familiar with Gettysburg, having graduated from Pennsylvania College as valedictorian of the Class of 1850. He had been taken prisoner on July 3 and sent to the Twelfth Corps field hospital to the rear of the Union lines, where he had been treated with much kindness and consideration. One of his former college professors, Professor Martin Stoever, accidentally discovered Crocker on a visit to this hospital, and the two happily shared a discussion of the old college days.

After a few days recuperating, Crocker, feeling self-conscious about his shabby suit of gray pants and jacket, decided to make an effort to obtain fresh clothing. He wrote to an old friend and former client, then living in Baltimore, for a loan. A few days later, two Sisters of Charity (a Catholic order) came to the hospital and asked to see Crocker, who later related, "They met me with gracious sympathy and kindness. One of them took me aside, and, unobserved, placed in my hand a package of money, saying it was from a friend, and requested no name be mentioned. They declined to give me any information. I never knew who they were. There was a mystery about them. They could not have come for my sake alone. But this I know, they were angels of mercy."

Crocker made known to the authorities his wish to go to Gettysburg to get his new clothing. Col. Walton Dwight and the hospital authorities trusted Crocker and gave him a free pass to Gettysburg, with the sole condition that he present it at the Provost office there and have it countersigned. He went alone, unattended. On his way to town, Crocker stopped by the Eleventh Corps Hospital to see the wounded Brig. Gen. Lewis Armistead, who had been taken there. To his chagrin, he found that the general had recently died and was shown his freshly covered grave.

Arriving in Gettysburg, Crocker had his pass countersigned at the Provost office, which gave him the freedom to roam the town where he had spent his college years. He later wrote, "There were many federal officers and soldiers in the city. It was a queer, incongruous sight to see a rebel lieutenant in gray mingling in the crowd, and apparently at home. They could see, however, many of the principal citizens of the town cordially accosting, and warmly shaking by the hand, that rebel. I met so many old friends that I soon felt at home. As I was walking along the main street a prominent physician, Dr. Charles Horner, stopped me and renewed the old acquaintanceship. He pointed to a lady standing in a door not far away, and asked me who it was. I gave the name of Miss Kate Arnold, a leading belle of the college days. He said, 'She is my wife and she wants to see you.' There was a mutually cordial meeting. While standing in a group of old friends I felt a gentle tap on my shoulder from behind. It was my dear old professor of mathematics, Jacobs. He whispered to me in his kindest, gentlest way not to talk about the war. I deeply appreciated his kindness and solicitude. But I had not been talking about the war. The war was forgotten as I talked of the olden days.

On another street a gentleman approached me and made himself known. It was Rev. David Swope, a native of Gettysburg, who was of the class next below mine. He manifested genuine pleasure in meeting me. He told me he was living in Kentucky when the war broke out. He recalled a little incident of the college days. He asked me if I remembered in passing a certain house where I said to a little red-headed girl with abundant red curls, standing in front of her house, 'I'll give you a levy for one of those curls.' I told him that I remembered it as if it were yesterday. He said that little girl was now his wife; and that she would be delighted to see me. He took me to a temporary hospital where there were a large number of our wounded. He had taken charge of the hospital, and manifested great interest in them and showed them every tender care and kindness. I fancied that those Kentucky days had added something to the sympathy of his kind, generous nature towards our wounded; and when I took leave of him, I am sure the warm grasp of my hand told him, better than my words, of the grateful feelings in my heart."

Crocker bought his new clothes and returned as promised to the hospital to resume his status as a prisoner of war.

James F. Crocker, Prison Reminiscences. (Portsmouth, VA: W. A. Fiske, 1906).

**

For many of the wounded, death was a slow and painful process that could take days, or even weeks. One Confederate surgeon, left behind to tend to the wounded when Lee's army retired, pushed his way through a crowd of idle spectators at the Second Corps hospital. A severely wounded North Carolinian called in a feeble voice, "You are a Confederate surgeon, are you not?" Upon being reassured that was indeed the case, the Tar Heel nervously caught the doctor's arm and "in a manner very striking and very eloquent," uttered, "What do you think, doctor? I am wounded and dying in defence of my country, and these people [the Union guards, doctors and onlookers] are trying to persuade me to take the oath of allegiance to theirs!" The crowd of Northerners scattered "as if a bomb had fallen in their midst." The doctor bowed in silence over the dying man, whose loyalty to the Southern cause transcended his captors' requests for reconciliation.

Frank Moore, Anecdotes, Poetry, and Incidents of the War: North and South. 1860-1865. (New York: Publication office, Bible house, J. Porteus, agent, 1867).

**

Another stricken Southerner summoned enough strength to write a final letter home to his family:

Battle-field, Gettysburg, July 4, 1863.

Dear Mother: I am here a prisoner of war, and mortally wounded. I can live but a few hours, at farthest. I was shot fifty yards from the enemy's line. They have been exceedingly kind to me. I have no doubt as to the final result of this battle, and I hope to live long enough to hear the shouts of victory before I die. I am very weak. Do not mourn my loss. I had hoped to have been spared; but a righteous God has ordered it otherwise, and I feel prepared to trust my case in his hands. Farewell to you all! Pray that God may receive my soul.

Your unfortunate son,

John

Frank Moore, Anecdotes, Poetry, and Incidents of the War: North and South. 1860-1865. (New York: Publication office, Bible house, J. Porteus, agent, 1867).

**

All over the battlefield, crews of soldiers and captured Confederates wearily dug graves and burial trenches and normally without ceremony, interred the dead. People from all over the countryside had flocked to Gettysburg to see the battlefield; some on foot, some on horseback and others via carriage or wagon. At one point, hundreds had gathered to watch Michael Shroyer and his comrades of the 147th Pennsylvania at this gruesome task. Disgusted by the voyeurism, a number of the soldiers collected guns from the field, loaded them, and suddenly fired a volley while screaming that the Rebels were coming. The crowd hurriedly raced for cover and did not return. Within a few minutes, the soldiers resumed their grim task, relieved that the dead at least had some privacy instead of being an exhibition.

M. S. Shroyer, History of Company G, 147th Regiment Volunteer Infantry, Snyder County Historical Society Bulletins, (Volume II, Number 2, 1939).

**

One hospital housed a number of soldiers of German ancestry. When one died, his comrades suggested that a particular German chaplain officiate at the burial. A grave was dug and those comrades well enough accompanied the body to its final resting place. The chaplain intoned with a deep accent, "Mine frens, dis ish the first time dis man had died." Observing a titter among his audience (many of whom were not German or even believers), he began again in Christian severity, "Mine frens, dis ish the first time dis man had died." Human nature took over, and some of the boys shouted as they could bear it no more. Indignant at the lack of respect given to him as a minister, the chaplain turned around, pointed at the empty grave and allegedly uttered, "Stick him in!" as he angrily marched away.

Frank Moore, Anecdotes, Poetry, and Incidents of the War: North and South. 1860-1865. (New York: Publication office, Bible house, J. Porteus, agent, 1867).

**

Following the fighting at Gettysburg, a large number of looters and relic collectors swarmed onto the still festering battlefield, openly taking guns, swords, accoutrements, and other military and personal effects. According to contemporary accounts, "a number of nondescript scavengers of mixed nationalities" from the Spring Forge region of southwestern

York County were persistent in traveling some 24 miles to the battlefield, collecting rags and clothing by the wagonload, and driving back caravan-style to the small hamlet. There, they sold their contraband to the Jacob Hauer paper mill, operated by a Philadelphia firm contracted by his heirs following Hauer's death in 1853. Since its founding in 1852, the single-machine mill on the Codorus Creek had been supplied by these vagabond peddlers, who had provided a cheap, but legal source of cotton fiber for the 1,500 pounds of paper produced each day. However, the raw material supply had dwindled during the Civil War as fabric had been diverted to the war effort. Now, with the debris of battle not far away, the rag dealers were harvesting a windfall of discarded clothing, bandages, and slings.

The scavengers did not endear themselves to the local populace. According to one eyewitness, "They even resurrected corpses from the shallow entombment in the hope that some valuables might be found on the festering body." Militia cavalry and infantry soon patrolled the Gettysburg area to prevent recurrences of such theft. Two weeks after the battle, a squad of 21st Pennsylvania cavalrymen accosted a trio of these rag dealers as they were departing for Spring Forge with their latest haul. They were quickly escorted back to Gettysburg, turned over to the provost marshal and summarily punished for their transgression of public orders against looting.

In particular, the thieves were ordered to dispose of the rotting remains of dead horses that still littered the battlefield. Some estimates suggest as many as 5,000 horses died during the battle, making the task of their disposal arduous and lengthy. The Confederate prisoners of war and local farmers who had been clearing the fields of these bodies were relieved to now have another source of captive labor. The prisoners were forced to unhitch their teams from the wagons. Using ropes and chains, they used their draft animals to drag the dead military horses into piles, which were then lit on fire to cremate the carcasses. The foul stench soured the air for miles. In several cases, the erstwhile peddlers also dug pits and buried the horses

"The dose the rag gatherers received was an ample sufficiency to give them the shivers from all future life at the barest glimpse of a blue uniform," wrote one resident. "Their plunder was confiscated, their teams and they themselves put to work. The work they did was hard work; it was menial and repulsive work; but there were glittering bayonets to enforce activity and diligence in their tasks. It was a long time before the trio ever saw Spring Forge. When they did they were sadder men; likewise wiser. They had lost all desire for battlefield plunder."

Their supply of contraband rags now cut off by the military and with the supply of clean rags and clothing diverted to the Camp Letterman military hospital for the wounded, the paper mill sank into insolvency. On December 23, 1863, the 101-acre complex was sold for $14,000 at an Orphans' Court sale to Philip Henry Glatfelter, a York Countian who had seven years of experience at a Maryland paper mill owned by his future father-in-law. The greatly expanded Spring Forge (now Spring Grove) mill is still operational as a key part of the current Glatfelter paper company.

Harrisburg Telegraph, September 20, 1907.

Many Gettysburg citizens had suffered financially and emotionally from the long ordeal. Two families, the Harmons and the Blisses, had seen their houses and barns deliberately destroyed to avoid their usage by sharpshooters, while Joseph Sherfy's barn near the now famous Peach Orchard had burned (killing many wounded soldiers) after a direct hit from an artillery shell. Hundreds of others experienced damage of various degrees. For one "poor, old, frowsy German woman," even the presence of the commanding general of the Army of the Potomac had not prevented her household from damage, nor did it ever gain her a penny in recompense. The widow Leister owned a small white frame house along Taneytown Road, which Meade had used as his headquarters. Her house was sadly shattered, and she bitterly complained (for years) of her losses. She later told author G. J. Gross, "When I comes home, my house was all over blood; the 'sogers' took away all my coverlits and quilts, two tons of hay, they spiled my spring, my apple-trees and every ding." She remarked that a couple hundred dollars would be of great help to her, and she should get it from "someveres."

Frank Moore, Anecdotes, Poetry, and Incidents of the War: North and South. 1860-1865. (New York: Publication office, Bible house, J. Porteus, agent, 1867).

There were tens of thousands of Federal soldiers still in Gettysburg on July 5, many with hunger and cravings, as well as cash. Some of the youths in Gettysburg found enterprising ways to take a portion of this money from the soldiers' purses. During the morning, Gus Bentley met his friend Daniel Skelly on the street and eagerly informed him that there was a large supply of tobacco at his place of employment, the Hollinger warehouse. "We hid it away before the Rebs came into town," he informed his chum, "and they did not find it. We can buy it and take it out and sell it to the soldiers." Like most boys of those days, they had little spending money to invest in the scheme. Daniel managed to talk his mother into a loan of ten dollars, and soon, Gus had done the same with his family. They eagerly marched down to the warehouse, plunked down their money, and purchased tobacco at wholesale pricing. It was in the form of large plugs – "Congress" tobacco, a well known brand at that time. With an old-fashioned tobacco cutter, the boys quickly cut it up into ten-cent pieces. Each of them filled a basket with the cut plugs, and then they headed out Baltimore Street to Evergreen Cemetery, the nearest line of battle.

Reaching the graveyard, they were turned back by artillery pickets, who had strict orders not to allow anyone to leave the town. Undaunted by this setback in reaching the main lines, the lads retreated into town. They headed eastward on High Street past the town's jail, where they turned onto a dirt path leading down to the "old Rock Creek swimmin hole." On the first ridge, they saw their first dead Confederate soldiers lying directly on the well worn path, two of them side by side. They followed the trail past Menchey's Spring, where it turned towards Culp's Hill. Ascending at one of its steepest points, the boys noted all kinds of battle scattered over the hillside, but the dead or wounded soldiers had already been removed. They finally reached the Federal breastworks, three-foot high rows of trees that had been cut down by the soldiers for protection from Confederate fire. Informed of the Gettysburg teenagers' intentions, the appreciative soldiers helped them over the breastworks with their baskets and the much anticipated cargo of fresh cut tobacco.

In a short time, both Dan and Gus had emptied their baskets and filled their pockets with coins. Business was so brisk that the soldiers encouraged them to go home and get more tobacco; they would buy all they could bring out to the hill. The enterprising boys made a number of round trips, selling out each time. After disposing of all their supply and paying back their borrowed capital, they each had more money than they could have dreamed.

Daniel Skelly "A Boy's Experiences During the Battle of Gettysburg" (Gettysburg: 1932). Files of the Gettysburg National Military Park.

**

In some cases, the days of persistent rumors and growing fear, followed by the actual destruction and stress caused by the Confederates' occupation of the region, was too much for the residents. Chambersburg farmer Absalom Shetter had seen his woodlot used to shelter Robert E. Lee's personal headquarters for two days. Thousands of troops had passed by his farm, located a half a mile from downtown. Many had stopped and procured whatever supplies and forage they could carry away. For Shetter, the shock of losing nearly all his livelihood was too much. He fretted for days about the losses and his uncertain future. The Sunday after the Battle of Gettysburg, he committed suicide. "The rebels had carried away all his stock and grain, and his mind became totally impaired. He was found hanging in the orchard, whither he had wandered during the night. As soon as he was discovered, an inquest was summoned by Esquire Hamman, who returned a verdict of death by hanging." He was buried the next day.

Valley Spirit, July 8, 1863.

**

Aging Chambersburg resident William Heyser was one of thousands of people who suffered financial damage as a result of the Confederate invasion. He walked out to his farm on July 2 to assess the damage. He discovered that there were holes cut in his fences everywhere, and his grain had been trampled as nearly 4,000 Rebels had camped on his farm. Forty acres of oats were gone, as well as much of his other crops. A "great stench" pervaded the woodlots and fields where the Rebels had camped. His house had been broken into and all clothing, food, and equipment useful to the Confederates were now missing. Two Rebels were discovered hiding in a barn. Heyser wanted to take them into town as prisoners, but, spotting nearby Confederate cavalry, he instead advised the duo of deserters to stay hidden. Later, one of the grateful Rebels gave Heyser a bayonet as a souvenir to thank him. An observant Heyser noted, "Most of our birds have gone since the appearance of the Rebels, and that flies and insects are more numerous."

Jane Dice Stone, ed., The Kittochtinny Historical Society Papers 16 (Mercersburg, Pennsylvania: Kittochtinny Historical Society, 1978)

**

Some soldiers in Lee's army knew they had suffered a serious setback. Hundreds deserted and many ended up staying in Pennsylvania, avoiding detection and in some cases eventually marrying local girls and raising families. Others fled northward towards Canada, in some cases aided by citizens (to the chagrin of Union Maj. Gen. Darius Couch, who bitterly complained about this act of disloyalty). Still, there were plenty of Confederate stragglers and prisoners to be processed.

As the 27th Pennsylvania Volunteer Militia slowly pursued Lee's army, they marched from Carlisle towards Gettysburg. On Monday, July 6, the emergency militiamen had time to freshen up before resuming their endless march toward the Mason-Dixon line at 8:00 a.m. Newspaper editor and temporary soldier Lt. Francis B. Wallace, while making his morning ritual in a mill stream next to the regiment's campsite, was amused at the tedious care with which a Rebel prisoner took with his own toilet. "He had a toothbrush, nicely scented soap, towel, etc., and he was a particular with his hair, teeth, nails, and other parts of his person as if he was preparing to participate in a grand reception at the court of his rebel master. He was cool, collected, and apparently, perfectly satisfied that he would be treated well."

Pottsville Miner's Journal, October 24, 1863

**

For most Confederates, morale remained high and Gettysburg was but a minor setback. Some even believed that they had won a tactical victory. Sir Arthur Fremantle, the British military observer, noted that "the road was full of soldiers marching in a particularly lively manner—the wet and mud seemed to have produced no effect whatever on their spirits, which were as boisterous as ever. They had got hold of colored prints of Mr. Lincoln, which they were passing about from company to company with many remarks upon the personal beauty of Uncle Abe. The same old chaff was going on: 'Come out of that hat—I know you're in it—I sees your legs a-dangling down.' "

Sir Arthur James Lyon Fremantle, Three Months in the Southern States: April, June, 1863. (Mobile: S. H. Goetzel, 1864)

**

Another Confederate had not lost his sense of wry humor. Back in late June, his regiment had stopped at Fayetteville to rest on the march from Chambersburg to Gettysburg. He and several other privates called on the hotel of a local named John Brown and demanded ale. Their host stated that he had just run out of that particular article. One of the Rebels retorted that they were going to Baltimore, where they would get plenty of mead and ale. Now, as the Confederates retreated on South Mountain, Brown by chance happened to meet this same once arrogant Rebel. He sarcastically asked if the soldier had ever got his Baltimore ale. "No," sadly replied the Johnny Reb, "we only got as far as Gettysburg, where the Meade was too strong for us, so we had to give up the Baltimore Ale." With that, he walked off, shuffling back towards Virginia.

Richard Miller, The Pictorial Book of Anecdotes and Incidents of the War of the Rebellion, Civil, Military, Naval and Domestic... (Hartford, CT: Hartford Publishing Company, 1867).

**

Sixteen-year-old Lida Welsh was a resident of Waynesboro, Pennsylvania, just north of the Mason-Dixon Line. She and the other citizens expected the worst as the Confederates streamed back through town en route to Maryland, but although the soldiers entered stores and took what they could carry away, as a general rule private property was not molested. She related, "The only exception to the rule was that they helped themselves to hats from citizens' heads and compelled some to sit on horse-blocks or curbs and take off their shoes or boots. One of our neighbors was a very decided Unionist, while his wife, a Virginian, gave her sympathy to the South. A barefoot soldier asked her for shoes, and he was scarcely out of sight with all she could find when her husband came home bareheaded, barefooted, and in a towering rage. He had to go shoeless, for there were no shoes to be had in town for love or money."

The Outlook, June 25, 1925, account of Lida Welsh Bender.

**

When the Army of Northern Virginia was retreating from Gettysburg, a young lady named Ellen Detrich was sitting on the porch of her old Greencastle home with a supply of bandages to aid the wounded. When one of the Rebel soldiers to whom she offered assistance rudely spurned her aid in bitter terms, his commander ordered him to dismount from his horse and present it to Miss Detrich for his impudence. She begged that this not be done, but the officer insisted. Taking a pencil from his pocket, he wrote her a brief note stating that no one should ever take the horse from her, and signing the name of a Confederate major, gave it to her. The horse was a very handsome roan, a typical prancing steed which was named Pompey. The Detrich family used their gift horse for several years for all kinds of service, ranging from hauling an old cart to prancing in a parade.

Charles M. Detrich, paper read before the Kittochtinny Historical Society of Franklin County, June 28, 1926.

**

As the 53rd North Carolina passed through the Monterey Gap on South Mountain, some of the weary Tar Heels jumped up on an old hog pen to rest. Unable to support the weight, the wooden structure suddenly collapsed and several soldiers fell in. To their astonishment, they discovered several boxes of clothing, dresses, shawls, blankets, and other apparel within the debris. Being "a little fellow," Pvt. Lewis Leon crawled through some of the boys' legs and captured a coat. He wrote in his diary that evening, "If the fool citizen would have left his things in his house they would have been safe, but to put it in our way was too much for us to leave behind."

L. Leon, Diary of a Tar Heel Confederate Soldier (Charlotte, NC: Stone Publishing Co., 1913)

**

The Union army slowly pursued Lee towards Virginia. On July 8, the remnant of the 114th Pennsylvania, shattered near the Peach Orchard, marched through Frederick, Maryland, to the rousing cheers of New York militia on duty there. During the tiring trek southward, musician Frank Rauscher witnessed "the meanness of some of the 'loyal' farmers of Pennsylvania and Maryland." Suffering from an illness, he was compelled to fall in the rear of the column and soon became separated from his regiment for several days. Along with other stragglers and indisposed soldiers, he relied upon the local farmers for something to eat. Rauscher late wrote, "They charged us fifty cents for a canteen of milk, and one dollar for a loaf of bread. One of these hay-seeders boasted of having made fifty dollars on a single barrel of flour, which was worked into bread and sold to the soldiers. We gave these sharkish yeomen to understand that it served them right if they were sometimes robbed by our men."

Frank Rauscher, Music on the March, 1862 – '65, with the Army of the Potomac. 114th Regt. P. V., Collis' Zouaves. (Philadelphia: Press of Wm. F. Fell & Co., 1892).

**

The First Army Corps marched back through Emmitsburg in northern Maryland, before taking a westerly route through beautiful farming country towards Hagerstown. Lt. Francis Wiggin was one of only about forty men remaining in the 16th Maine, a regiment sacrificed on July 1 in a desperate attempt to buy time to allow Robinson's division to escape to Cemetery Hill. Now, as the little band of weary troopers marched along, they were quiet as they mourned the loss of their comrades, with over 150 now headed southward to Confederate prisons. Wiggins later related, "As we passed a turn in the road we came to a beautiful house in the midst of well kept grounds, the whole enclosed by a broad, low stone wall. On this wall, near the road, stood a young lady dressed in white, and around her, stood a dozen younger misses, also dressed in white, all waving United States flags, and singing the 'Battle Cry of Freedom,' that stirring battle song, which had just been published. This was the first time we had ever heard it, and perhaps you can imagine the effect of the words, as sung by these young ladies, on the little remnant of the Sixteenth Maine, whose flag had been torn up to save it from capture, only four days before. As moved by a common impulse, every man came to a halt and removed his cap. When the song was concluded there was not ... They could not cheer the singers, but silently they moved on ... young ladies were no longer in view. I think the elder young ... ttle band passed from her view, she dipped her flag toward them

h Maine Regiment at Gettysburg, War Papers, Maine MOLLUS, 0.

**

members of the 3rd Michigan found that the most threatening ... ates they were pursuing, but the local guardians of food supplies. ... some honey, raided some beehives in a nearby garden, initially ... ver, as the men reached the hives, the bees counterattacked en ... e men as they struggled to get away from the prolonged assault. ... Sgt. Daniel Crotty, later wrote that the slashing and darting bees ... somersaulting on the ground as to put to shame a lot of Japanese ... us ring." The soldiers made an inglorious retreat, their swollen ... bling huge mortar shells. Crotty added, "So I think they will be ... his, and leave their bees alone."

Campaigning in the Army of the Potomac, (Grand Rapids, MI:

**

back to Virginia were filled with Confederates, most still in ... nation. A reporter in Greencastle, Pennsylvania, witnessed the ... and the wounded as they passed through town on July 8. He ... lowed by "five to ten thousand stragglers on foot, most of them ... them in the mud. Many had their shirt sleeves torn off for ... hat, others with heads tied up, others with one leg of their ... this some six to ten thousand mounted infantry and cavalry on ... ling in the mud, with here and there a stray piece of artillery, and the wagons and ambulances, and you have some idea of the panorama as it moved along."

The First Army Corps marched back through Emmitsburg in northern Maryland, as before taking a westerly route through beautiful farming country towards Hagerstown. Lt. Francis Wiggin was one of only about forty men remaining in the 16th Maine, a regiment sacrificed on July 1 in a desperate attempt to buy time to allow Robinson's division to escape to Cemetery Hill. Now, as the little band of weary troopers marched along, they were quiet as they mourned the loss of their comrades, with over 150 now headed southward to Confederate prisons. Wiggins later related, "As we passed a turn in the road we came to a beautiful house in the midst of well kept grounds, the whole enclosed by a broad, low stone wall. On this wall, near the road, stood a young lady dressed in white and around her stood

a dozen younger misses, also dressed in white, all waving United States flags, and singing the 'Battle Cry of Freedom,' that stirring battle song, which had just been published. Thi

Lt. Francis Wiggin, Sixteenth Maine Regiment at Gettysburg, War Papers, Maine MOLLUS, Volume 4, December 7, 1910.

For 36 hours, the steady parade of tired Southern soldiers had passed through the small borough, wending their way towards the swollen Potomac River. The reporter continued, "Oh, what a scene! The teamsters with horrid oaths pounded the poor exhausted horses and mules, while the road was strewn with dead horses and broken wagons. Here and there you could see a team fast in the mud with men prying at it with rails, while by the wayside, against trees, stumps, and in the mud, sat the exhausted wounded unable to go any further. Thousands more fortunate than these poor wretches were endeavoring to make their escape on the worn-out horses which they had stolen, who when requested by some exhausted wretch to leave him ride for a few miles or so, would turn a deaf ear to the supplications of his companions in arms; for in the vortex and confusion all sense of feeling was lost. Misfortune had placed officers and privates on the same level. The stolen goods were freely exchanged for a small piece of bread or cake.

The road was strewn with cast-off clothing, blankets, knapsacks, guns and empty haversacks. But amid all the confusion and noise could be heard the moans of the wounded in the wagons and ambulances, as they were hurried over the rough, muddy roads. Many died on the way, and were thrown into the woods and barns for the citizens to bury. When a wagon would brake (sic) down, the wounded would be left to their fate. Oh, how they would beg and entreat those around them not to leave them there to die, far from their friends and homes! But their supplications and tears were lost upon men who, hardened by the misfortunes with which they were surrounded, made the old maxim 'self-preservation is the first law of nature,' their guide. When a team would give out or a horse become exhausted, they would lighten the wagon by throwing one or two of the wounded out, who, with tears in their eyes, would beg for mercy; but humanity had left the teamster, and he heard them not. Thousands of them would enquire, 'How far to the river?' 'How far to the Maryland line?' 'How far to Williamsport?' When answered that it was twenty miles to the river, they would look bewildered, and say 'I cannot walk that far.' Others would sit down, yielding calmly to their fate. Others again would beg for medical aid, but it was not to be had.

On the road you can see large quantities of ammunition - powder, shell and shot, which has been abandoned. In less than a half a mile I counted three dismounted guns. Whole wagon loads of small arms were burnt, or rendered useless by bending them over wagon wheels."

The reporter further noted that the Southern sympathizers in the region did not fare well. They had claimed protection from the Rebels on the grounds that they had voted for Southern Democrat John Breckinridge in the 1860 presidential election. However, the Confederates responded that they did not care who they had voted for, but instead inquired, "If you are for us, why not help us by falling into the ranks." Few, if any, did so. The Copperheads had learned a lesson, and were now good Union men.

Lancaster (PA) Daily Express, July 11, 1863

**

Finally, the retreating Confederate army reached the fords of the swollen Potomac River. At Williamsport, a large train of supply wagons huddled in a deep hollow or depression on the north side of the river, waiting for the water level to fall low enough for safe passage to Virginia. Federal cavalry approached, and horse artillery soon unlimbered and shelled the river banks as Edward Johnson's Rebel infantry waded across. A Southern quartermaster officer approached the array of parked wagons and was amazed to discover that all the teamsters were missing. His wonder as to their whereabouts was soon solved. He happened to look at the river, where he saw hundreds of heads just showing above the water. The teamsters had with one accord plunged into the river to escape the hurtling shells, and they were now submerged to the neck.

Randolph H. McKim, A Soldier's Recollections: Leaves from the Diary of a Young Confederate. (New York: Longmans, Green, and Co., 1910).

**

One evening, several soldiers from the 25th Virginia were detailed to go into Williamsport, Maryland, and bake a large quantity of bread for the regiment. On the edge of the town, John King and Bill Lawhorne from Company B discovered several barrels of flour hidden in a shed in a lumberyard. Not having any utensils to properly prepare and bake the bread, the veteran soldiers instead improvised. Lawhorne spread an oilcloth on the ground, piled flour out of the barrel on it, put salt and soda in the dough and mixed it while his companion built a fire. King then gathered pieces of barrel heads and scraps of boards and placed on the ground. Lawhorne spread the dough out on them and placed the boards in front of the now roaring fire. When one side of the dough was cooked, King turned the cake over and baked the other side. The pair soon had a fine lot of bread, which "certainly tasted good to us for we weren't troubled with gout on account of luxurious living." While King was busy baking, Lt. Gen. A. P. Hill's corps passed along the road by the fire, so the two Virginians had to continually watch their steaming bread to prevent pilferage, although one hungry Third Corps soldier managed to steal one of King's best cakes.

The night was very dark and rainy. Toward morning, someone informed the soldiers that their regiment was passing through the town. King and Lawhorne rapidly packed the bread so they could conveniently carry it. They waded through the darkness in the deepening mud until they found their regiment. On reaching the upper end of Williamsport, they could see a long line of men wading across the Potomac River. King narrated, "It was just break of day and it was terrible to see the men in the big river with only their heads above water, but we joined them and continued our march. Orders had been given that the ammunition be kept dry. I placed the cartridge box upon my shoulder and held my load of bread as high above the water as possible. The boys cried out: 'For God's sake King, take care of the bread.' It was not surprising that they were uneasy about the bread as the water came to the level of my shoulders…However, we crossed safely. The Potomac was rising rapidly when we waded but the water was warm. We rejoiced to be again on Virginia's soil."

John R. King, My Experience in the Confederate Army and in Northern Prisons. (Clarksburg, WV: Stonewall Jackson Chapter, United Daughters of the Confederacy, 1917).

**

Finally, Lee's battered army had crossed the Potomac into Virginia and relative safety, as Meade did not aggressively follow up his victory. To many defiant Confederates, Gettysburg was but a temporary setback, and in many cases, morale was still quite high. Maj. Gen. Jubal Early believed, "Our army was not at all demoralized, and calmly awaited the attack of the enemy. My own division was buoyant and defiant, for it felt that it had sustained no defeat, and though diminished in numbers it was as ready to fight the enemy as at Gettysburg." Lt. Joseph Hilton of the 26th GA wrote, "I am once more in Dixie, safe and sound, and ready for anything that may turn up, either to move forward, or backward, run or fight, or anything else Robert E. Lee tells me to do."

Jubal Anderson Early C. S. A., Autobiographical Sketch and Narrative of the War Between the States. (Philadelphia and London: J. B. Lippinscott Company, 1912).

Joseph Hilton letters, Gettysburg National Military Park

**

General Lee had left behind thousands of seriously wounded men who could not be safely moved or that had been left behind enemy lines as prisoners. Among the former was 18-year-old Sgt. David Johnston of the 7th Virginia Infantry in Pickett's Division. During the July 3 cannonade, he had hugged the ground in the welcome shade of an apple tree, trying to escape the shells crashing in from the distant Union lines. He and his comrades buried their faces as deep into the sod as possible. When Johnston finally raised his head to draw a breath of fresh air, a nearby lieutenant remarked, "You had better put your head down or you may get it knocked off." Johnston replied: "A man had about as well die that way as to suffocate for want of air."

Near the end of the lengthy barrage, a Federal gun on Cemetery Hill found the range and began lofting shells towards the huddled masses of Kemper's Brigade. One bounding shot sheared off the heads of a pair of Confederates before exploding and wounding Johnston and two others. Johnston found that his ribs were fractured, his left lung contused, and his left side and limbs paralyzed. He was propped up against the apple tree and left behind as the division advanced. He recalled a premonition from the march from Chambersburg to Gettysburg that he would be hit in the left shoulder by an artillery shell and left for dead. The depressed Johnston was carried to the Spangler Woods, where regimental surgeons stabilized him. After dark, an ambulance hauled the prostrated Confederate to the shed of a farmer's barn, near the house where the wounded General Kemper had been taken.

After a couple of restless days, a friend helped fix a shelter and a bed for Johnston in the farmer's orchard, where he was away from the ghastly sounds and sights of the amputations, the dying, and the men out of their minds with pain and grief. As the Confederates withdrew on July 4, Maj. Gen. Jubal Early, accompanied by Kemper's brigade surgeon, passed among the men, encouraging as many as could to climb into wagons for the trip to Virginia. Still partially paralyzed, Johnston stayed put and was captured by the Federal advance guard not long after the last wagons had departed. A Federal doctor examined Johnston and left instructions that he was not to be given solid food, but only lemonade and spirits. A Union soldier from Ohio became Johnston's nurse as his wounds healed and the paralysis eased. The Yankee delighted in reading the Philadelphia newspapers to his stricken foe, particularly articles regarding Meade's pursuit of Lee's retreating army and the expectation that he would be forced to surrender or be destroyed. The Buckeye's countenance fell on July 13 when he read news that Lee has successfully escaped into Virginia and the war would continue.

Johnston would be able to walk (aided by a Union captain) to the Gettysburg train station on July 20 for the long trip to Baltimore, where he and his comrades were taken under guard to a fenced-in area of a hospital. Soldiers kept back a crowd of women and onlookers that tried to give the Rebels food and encouragement, and when the well-wishers threw food over the high fence, the Yankee guards used their bayonets to prevent the wounded Confederates from partaking of it. He was later moved by boxcar to a hospital in Chester, Pennsylvania, where he was paroled a month later and sent home on furlough. After being exchanged in November, he rejoined his regiment, much to the surprise of his comrades who had given him up for dead.

David E. Johnston, The Story of a Confederate Boy in the Civil War. (Portland, OR: Glass & Prudhomme Company, 1914).

**

The wounded Confederates still at Gettysburg elicited many responses from their hosts, ranging from deep sympathy and concern to scorn and derision. In one case, it was curiosity that sparked an amusing incident. One particular farmer who lived about 5 miles from the battlefield had never seen a Rebel. Three weeks after the fighting, he rode into town to find some. He came to Camp Letterman (a military hospital established just east of Gettysburg to treat soldiers until they could be removed via train to more permanent locations) and stated his intention to see a Rebel. The nurses unceremoniously ushered him into a tent and announced, "Boys, here's a man who never saw a rebel in his life, and wants to look at you." The amazed farmer stood there with his mouth agape as he viewed the rows of Rebels reclining on their beds. They laughed at the "stupid old Dutchman" who seemed not to know what now to do. One of the visiting lady nurses inquired of the man, "And why haven't you seen a rebel? Why didn't you take your gun and help to drive them out of your town?" He unthinkingly replied, "A feller might'er get hit." That was too much for the Confederates, who now uncontrollably roared with laughter at him, up and down the tent. The dumbfounded man slipped away quietly, his encounter with the Rebels not having went the way he had anticipated.

Frank Moore, Anecdotes, Poetry, and Incidents of the War: North and South. 1860-1865. (New York: Publication office, Bible house, J. Porteus, agent, 1867).

**

The work of identifying the dead and caring for the wounded at Gettysburg continued for months. Anxious families visited Gettysburg, or posted inquiries in papers and through letters and friends, looking for information regarding missing loved ones. Likewise, the wounded soldiers tried to get messages back home. In one poignant story, W. N. Phelps had said goodbye to his wife and six-year-old daughter in Columbus, Georgia to join the Confederate army in 1861. A member of the 18th Georgia, he survived several battles, but was grievously wounded in the head at Gettysburg and left for dead. Reports incorrectly circulated that he had been killed, but in actuality, he was slowly recovering in a Federal hospital as a prisoner of war. He escaped, but could not make his way through Union lines to return to the South, and instead, booked passage on a ship to Costa Rica in Central America, where he found employment constructing a railroad.

After the war, he returned to Georgia, but could not locate any of his family members. His mother had died, believing him to have perished at Gettysburg, and he heard rumors that his wife and little girl had moved to Alabama. Phelps searched in vain for quite some time, including placing advertisements in leading newspapers. Heartbroken, he returned to Costa Rica where for the next 37 years he served as an engineer on a government railroad.

Upon his retirement in 1907, he came back to the United States and settled near Birmingham, Alabama, still hoping to locate his daughter. He placed ads in local papers, as well as one in his hometown of Columbus, Georgia. Amazingly, a hotel owner named Captain Affleck read the Columbus ad and recognized his wife's maiden name as the woman being sought by the old Confederate. He took a train to Alabama to inform Phelps that indeed his daughter was still alive, although now a grandmother. Together, the two men returned to Columbus, where the 74-year-old Gettysburg veteran had a touching reunion with the daughter he had not seen since 1861.

The Roanoke (Alabama) Leader, March 13, 1907.

**

Gettysburg was the bloodiest battle ever fought in the United States. For three days, over 150,000 men had contested the fields, roads and hills surrounding the Adams County seat. One third of the combatants were counted as casualties, but thousands more suffered from psychological trauma, physical illnesses, sunstroke and heat exhaustion, and other ailments as a result of the campaign and battle. For many of the wounded and ill, the aftereffects would linger until death claimed the old veterans. The civilians also suffered emotional distress, as well as in some cases, financial ruin. Gettysburg had been transformed from an unknown sleepy Pennsylvania rural town into a world-famous destination.

Efforts began almost immediately to preserve large tracts of land, as well as to construct a National Cemetery for the Union dead. In November of 1863, President Abraham Lincoln arrived in town to say a few words during the lengthy dedication ceremony for the new cemetery, on a site adjacent to the borough's Evergreen Cemetery. His brief remarks remain a fitting and timeless memorial to those men who fought at Gettysburg, perhaps far more eternal than the stone and bronze monuments that commemorate many of the actions depicted in this book.

Four score and seven years ago our fathers brought forth on this continent, a new nation, conceived in Liberty, and dedicated to the proposition that all men are created equal.

Now we are engaged in a great civil war, testing whether that nation, or any nation so conceived and so dedicated, can long endure. We are met on a great battle-field of that war. We have come to dedicate a portion of that field, as a final resting place for those who here gave their lives that that nation might live. It is altogether fitting and proper that we should do this.

But, in a larger sense, we can not dedicate–we can not consecrate–we can not hallow–this ground. The brave men, living and dead, who struggled here, have consecrated it, far above our poor power to add or detract. The world will little note, nor long remember what we say here, but it can never forget what they did here. It is for us the living, rather, to be dedicated here to the unfinished work which they who fought here have thus far so nobly advanced. It is rather for us to be here dedicated to the great task remaining before us–that from these honored dead we take increased devotion to that cause for which they gave the last full measure of devotion–that we here highly resolve that these dead shall not have died in vain– that this nation, under God, shall have a new birth of freedom–and that government of the people, by the people, for the people, shall not perish from the earth.

About the Author

Scott L. Mingus, Sr. is a scientist and executive in the paper and printing industry, and holds patents in self-adhesive postage stamp products and in bar code labels. He is the author of several books on wargaming the Civil War, including the two-volume "Enduring Valor: Gettysburg in Miniature," the popularly acclaimed "Undying Courage: The Antietam Campaign in Miniature," and "Crossed Sabers: Gettysburg in Miniature." He and his wife Debi are the editors and publishers of "Charge!," an international magazine for Civil War miniature wargamers. He has also written historical articles for several other magazines. His latest work, "My Brother's Keeper," will be published in 2007 with over a dozen new wargaming scenarios for the Gettysburg campaign for skirmish-level wargaming.

A native of southern Ohio, he attended Miami University in Oxford, Ohio, completing his undergraduate degree in Paper Science and Engineering in 1978. He is married to Deborah (Ferrell) Mingus, and they have three adult children and a grandson, Tristan. Mingus spent 23 years working for office products giant Avery Dennison before joining the P. H. Glatfelter Company, a global manufacturer of specialty papers, in 2001.

Scott and Debi Mingus now reside in York, Pennsylvania, and attend the Stillmeadow Church of the Nazarene. He can be reached at scottmingus@yahoo.com.

****

<u>Other Books by Colecraft</u>

Civil War Artillery at Gettysburg
by Philip M. Cole

ISBN 0-9777125-08

Command and Communication Frictions in the Gettysburg Campaign
by Philip M. Cole

ISBN 0-9777125-16

Human Interest Stories from Antietam
by Scott L. Mingus, Sr.

ISBN 0-9777125-32

Visit us at: www.colecraftbooks.com

e-mail us at: colecraftbooks@aol.com

Printed in the United States
203819BV00002B/179-262/A